Rock
Climbing

The Starting Series

Rock Climbing

ARTHUR B. CLARKE

illustrations by Ian A. R. Price

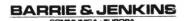

BARRIE & JENKINS
COMMUNICA · EUROPA

Dedication

to the UPA

First published in 1979 by
Barrie & Jenkins Limited
24 Highbury Crescent, London N5 1RX

ISBN   0 214 20488 X (cased)
       0 214 20618 1 (paperback)

Typeset by Computacomp (UK) Ltd, Fort William, Scotland

Printed in Great Britain by litho by
The Anchor Press Ltd and bound by
Wm Brendon & Son Ltd, both of
Tiptree, Essex

Frontispiece: Napes Needle, Great Cable, Cumbria

Acknowledgements

Acknowledgement is due to the following:

Messrs Bob and Ellis Brigham of Ellis Brigham, Manchester, climbing equipment specialists, for valuable assistance, especially in the loan of equipment;

Harold Woolley and John Allen of the Rucksack Club for reading the manuscript and offering helpful advice and criticism;

Rachel Clarke for typing the manuscript;

John Jackson for writing the Foreword;

John Cleare for providing the jacket illustration.

Finally I would specifically like to thank all my friends, members of the Rucksack Club and all the staff, past and present, of Plas y Brenin who are probably unaware of their contribution but have been fundamental in developing my appreciation of the mountains and in shaping my approach to the teaching of rock climbing. I would also like to express my appreciation to Dave Alcock for permission to use certain material.

Craig y Dderwen
Maenan

ARTHUR CLARKE
1978

Foreword

During 1945 I was the Chief Instructor at the RAF Mountaineering Centre in the Kashmir Himalaya. There I realised that introducing others to the fascination of mountaineering was a very satisfying experience and I also realised that it needed to be done well if the right attitudes, as well as the best techniques, were to be developed. Since those days I have had the fortune to gather together and work with some of the finest, most dedicated and clear-thinking teachers of rock climbing and mountaineering it is possible to acquire. The author of this book is one of them. His clarity of thought is allied to clarity of text and diagrams, so that with practical application the reader will quickly develop sound skills and sort out problems. The key to this clarity and to becoming a first-class teacher and mountaineer is experience, an experience which Arthur Clarke has acquired in abundance in Britain, the Alps, Greenland and the Himalaya.

It gives me great pleasure to recommend this book to those who seek the physical and mental refreshment of the mountains and the crags, and write the Foreword in the sure knowledge that all will benefit by climbing with a basis of sound methods and techniques.

John A. Jackson
February 1978
Director, 1960 – 1975
National Mountaineering Centre,
Plas y Brenin, North Wales.

Contents

	Foreword	6
	Introduction	8
1	Equipment	11
2	Learning to Climb	25
3	Climbing Technique	45
4	Knots	53
5	Belaying	61
6	Pitons and Chocks	79
7	Prusiking and Abseiling	93
8	Guide Books and Gradings	115
	Glossary	119
	Index	121

Introduction

CLIMBING

Climbing is instinctive. Young children do it spontaneously and naturally. There is an element of risk involved, an element of danger – all part of the attraction, the excitement of climbing.

In later life many venture onto rock faces, into quarries or onto sea cliffs. Whilst some people retain a natural ability to climb, others have to learn or re-learn the basic techniques.

Acquiring these basic techniques in no way eliminates the 'risk' element of the sport – an element that is important and indeed a fundamental attraction.

ABOUT THIS BOOK

This book introduces the basics of rock climbing to the beginner by adopting a visual approach and working on the premise that a carefully chosen picture will tell the story much more easily. Hence there is a profusion of illustrations throughout the book.

It must be admitted that no book can teach you to climb. Climbing is a practical skill which will only develop with experience and more experience. However, some basic knowledge is needed and we have tried to present this in *Rock Climbing*.

We have aimed to introduce the prospective climber to the minimum equipment he or she will require and to outline the basic skills necessary for 'safe' climbing.

As this book is part of *The Starting Series* it has been difficult to know what to put in and what to leave out. It may be asked, 'When does basic rock climbing become advanced?' The truth is that this will vary from individual to individual. We have tried therefore to include enough information to cover most needs and to avoid being dogmatic about equipment and method. We have also tried to point out advantages and disadvantages, so that the individual climber may decide for him/herself.

When the basic skills have been acquired and you have had some experience as a second, the next step is to start leading. The standard of the climb is not important except that it is better to start leading at a lower standard than that at which you have been seconding. The very fact of leading any climb means that you will be making the decisions, thereby increasing your confidence and skill and experiencing in full the challenge and excitement of rock climbing.

HOW TO START

Compared with times past, there are now numerous ways open to those who wish to learn to rock climb. Many still approach a friend to take them climbing and to explain the jargon and technicalities. This is a perfectly good way of learning, provided the friend is competent and well-experienced, and has the ability to pass on the skills. The prospective climber has a problem in that he/she is not in a position to judge whether the friend is competent or not.

This initial learning phase is very important. If the instruction is good then it is much easier for the learner to assimilate and build on it in order to gain competence and experience.

A highly recommended way of learning to climb is to seek professional instruction, of which there are various forms. In Britain the Sports Councils (Government Agencies) run rock climbing courses at their respective National Centres. Other agencies, climbing clubs and well known individual climbers run similar courses. The easiest way to obtain the addresses of any of these is to buy copies of climbing magazines and to read the advertisements.

In most countries with a history of mountaineering, professional Guides are available for hire. Their addresses are usually available from the local Guide Association secretary. It is possible to learn a great deal by employing a professional Guide. Besides having the experience and thrill of climbing a possibly otherwise unattainable route, the novice can watch the way the Guide climbs and deals with various technical situations.

Until comparatively recently rock climbing came under the general umbrella of mountaineering and it was traditional to spend some time acquiring the skills of hill walking and scrambling before moving on to rock climbing. This 'apprenticeship' has a lot to recommend it where rock climbing is undertaken on high mountain crags where skills other than climbing are required.

It was also traditional to start on the easiest climbs and to move up a grade only when the skills and techniques were mastered. It could be argued that this approach served to create artificial and psychological barriers of achievement between the various grades.

Today, rock climbing is a sport in its own right and the people taking it up have brought with them a refreshing wave of enthusiasm which together with modern sophisticated equipment and protection has helped to push the standard of rock climbing to a very high level of achievement.

Many of today's climbers approach the sport with an athlete's dedication that was generally unheard of twenty years ago. The development of specially designed climbing walls has allowed people to practise and train indoors. Indeed many of the people taking up the sport have been introduced to it through the medium of a climbing wall.

In Britain many of these 'new' climbers are young teenagers and their interest in rock climbing stems from the fact that in a great number of schools, outdoor activities are part of the basic school curriculum.

In conclusion we must emphasize that the only way to learn to climb is to go and do it.

GOOD CLIMBING!

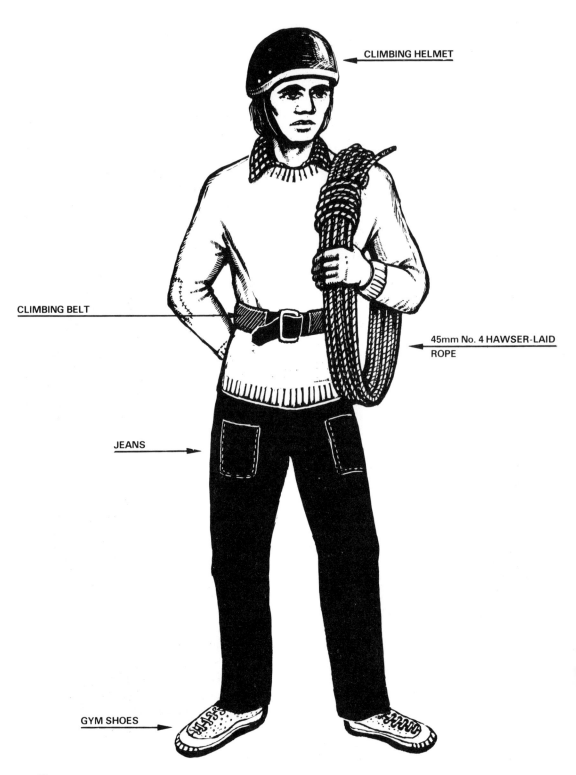

CLIMBING HELMET

CLIMBING BELT

45mm No. 4 HAWSER-LAID ROPE

JEANS

GYM SHOES

Chapter One: Equipment

Climbing equipment is very expensive and it is advisable not to rush straight off to the nearest shop until you have at least used and handled some equipment. Most retail stores issue very comprehensive catalogues and these are worth studying in detail.

Initially you will require little equipment and a suggested list is given at the end of this chapter. After tackling a few climbs and talking to other climbers you will be in a much better position to decide for yourself which items of equipment you will need to buy.

BOOTS

As a beginner, don't be tempted to buy specialist boots until you are sure that you intend to continue rock-climbing.

Initially, gym-shoes [a] or walking boots (known as 'bendy boots' to climbers – make sure they have a cleated *rubber* sole and not plastic) will be adequate for elementary climbing.

However, when you do come to buy a pair of boots for rock climbing, they will most likely be of one of the following types.

Climbing Boots
The uppers are leather and give support to the ankle although they are sometimes cut on the low side. They have a 'vibram'-type rubber sole [b] with an inner stiffening-plate. This enables the boot to be used on very small holds without bending and therefore helps to develop neat footwork.

They are close fitting and laced down to the toe for a tight fit [c]. The welt tends to be narrow. Having a rigid sole they are not really suitable for mountain walking.

On some outcrops, especially sandstone, the use of 'heavy' climbing-boots is not encouraged because of the wear they cause to the rock.

Specialist Rock-Climbing Boots
Lightweight rock-climbing boots (friction boots) were originally developed by Pierre Allain in the 1950s. There are several makes available today, such as PA's, EB's, or RD's. Initially this type of boot was only used by climbers for the harder routes but they are now the accepted footwear at all standards.

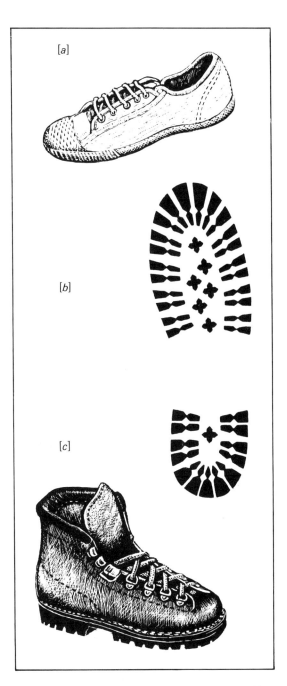

[a]

[b]

[c]

They have a smooth rubber sole which extends on to the upper [a] and [b]. This feature, called the 'rand', protects the upper from excessive abrasion and also assists when jamming the feet in cracks. The uppers are made of canvas or suede, with the lacing going right to the narrow toe, so that a tight fit can be achieved.

A word of warning: Special care should be taken when descending steep grass slopes, especially when wet, if wearing smooth-soled boots as there is a danger of slipping due to lack of friction.

Kletterschuhe

These lightweight climbing boots [c] were originally developed for climbing in the Dolomites. The uppers were made from backed suede with felt soles. The modern 'klet' has a lightweight cleated rubber sole. In Great Britain the kletterschuh has been replaced by the PA type.

When buying lightweight climbing boots, make sure that they are a close fit so that you can 'feel' the rock and they fit your foot shape. Some have stiffer soles than others and choice is dictated by personal climbing-style. Stiff soles are excellent for standing on small holds and jamming in cracks. Flexible soles are better for rounded holds and slab-climbing.

CLIMBING HELMETS (CRASH HATS, HARD HATS or BONE DOMES)

Whether to wear a climbing helmet [a, opposite] is the subject of much argument and discussion among climbers. Figures issued by the Mountain Rescue Committee of Great Britain indicate a reduction in head injuries reflecting the increased use of helmets in Britain. A helmet will give some protection from natural rock-falls, or more usually from loose rock or equipment dropped or dislodged by climbing parties. In the end, the individual must decide whether or not to wear a helmet. This should be a considered choice, and not one based upon current fashions or trends.

Helmets are usually made of fibreglass weighing 24–27 oz (680–770 g) with an energy-absorbing lining [b, opposite]. A helmet should give all-round protection, yet allow good head movement and all-round vision. Helmets are usually sold in various sizes or provided with an adjustable inner head band. Remember that you may wish to wear a Balaclava under the helmet in winter. The inner harness must be adjusted to suit the height of your crown. Some helmets are sold with an adjustable chin strap.

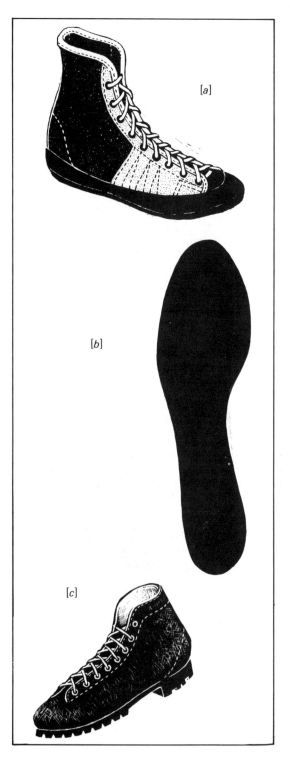

[a]

[b]

[c]

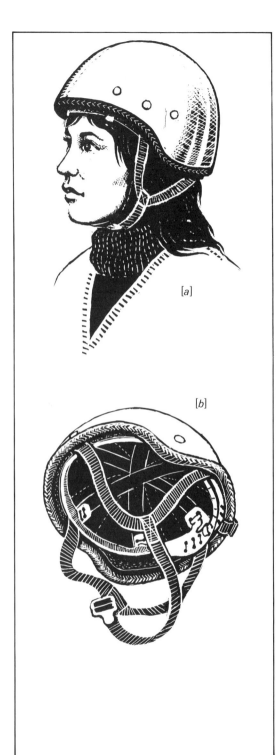

[a]

[b]

Ideally, helmets in Great Britain should comply with the requirements of BS 4423. In the United States the safest policy is to follow the standards recommended by the UIAA.

WAIST TIES

Belts and Harnesses
There are many methods of attaching the climbing rope to the body. The simplest and traditional way is to tie the end of the rope round the waist by means of the 'bowline' or 'figure-of-eight' knot [c].

Waistbelts
The basic idea of any belt or harness is to spread the possible load, in the event of a fall, over a larger area of the body than is possible with the rope tied directly round the waist. It also enables gear to be carried in a convenient manner.

[c]

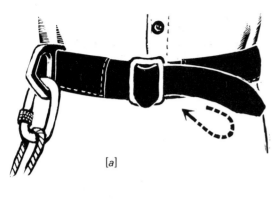

[a]

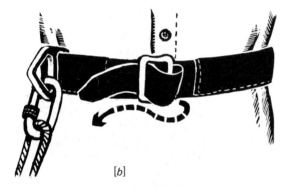

[b]

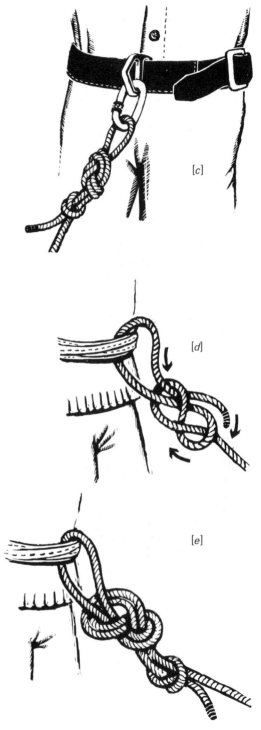

[c]

[d]

[e]

The most popular waist belt used in Britain is made by Troll from 2 in nylon webbing with a protective canvas sleeve closed by a buckle [a]. A floating 'D' ring gives variable rope attachment via a karabiner.

IT IS IMPERATIVE THAT THE TAIL OF THE BELT IS THREADED BACK THROUGH THE BUCKLE AS ILLUSTRATED [b].

It is recommended that the buckle is fastened at the side, and when you are climbing, the 'D' ring is at the front [c]. It can easily be floated to the back for belaying (see page 63).

Swami Belt

This belt is popular in the US and consists of 1 in nylon tape wrapped around the waist five or six times and tied with a ring bend or tape knot. The climbing rope is tied direct to the waist tie [d] and [e] by means of a figure-of-eight and thumb knot.

Sit Harnesses

Basically these harnesses are designed to take the weight behind the thighs in the event of a fall and are made up from stitched nylon webbing. The most popular model in Britain is one designed by Don Whillans.

When purchasing a 'Troll/Whillans' harness [a] and [b], it is important to buy one suited to your waist size and also to read the comprehensive leaflet issued with the harness.

Body Harnesses [c]

These are used extensively on the European continent and are gaining in approval in Britain. However, they do give a feeling of being trussed up and for this reason, many climbers find them too restrictive.

[a]

[b]

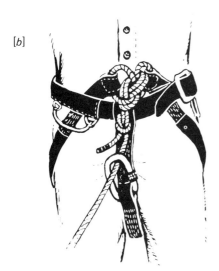

[c]

Improvised Chest Harness

This simple chest harness [a] is made up from a normal eight-foot tape sling passed over one arm and taken round the back and under the other arm. It is tied off with a sheet bend [b]. This harness could be linked to a waist belt or sit harness to make a form of full body harness.

CLIMBING ROPE

For climbing, it is recommended that ropes are made from synthetic fibre. Nylon and Perlon are trade names for very similar materials. One of the most important properties of nylon climbing rope is its ability to stretch when subjected to load. This extension will absorb energy if handled correctly,

[a]

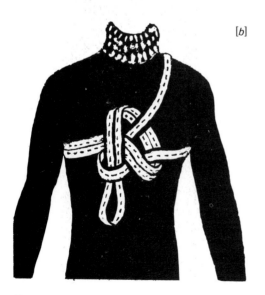

[b]

thus preventing the shock load from injuring the climber and damaging the rope.

Nylon rope is relatively light in weight, does not absorb water and will not rot if left damp. It is affected by acid and some chemicals so it must be stored carefully. Being a soft material it is subject to abrasion if it runs over a sharp edge or is dragged along the ground. Also it melts at a low temperature (heat of a match flame) which can very easily be achieved by friction of nylon running over nylon. ALWAYS bear this in mind while rock climbing.

Do not buy or use any rope sold for marine use or caving. These ropes have different physical properties and are not suitable for climbing. They could result in FATAL accidents.

Two types of rope construction are available to the climber.

Hawser-Laid (Twisted/Cable) Rope

This is the traditional method of rope-construction where fibres are twisted into strands and three strands are twisted around each other [a]. Rope of this construction in Britain should conform to BS 3104. It is recommended that No. 4 (11mm equivalent), $1^3/_4$ in circumference with a minimum breaking-strain of 4200lb (1905kg) be used for climbing.

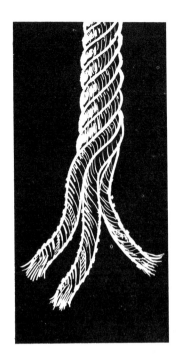

[a]

Table of Rope Size and Strength

Size	Breaking Strain
No. 1 (5mm)	1000lb (454kg)
No. 2 (7mm)	2000lb (907kg)
No. 3 (10mm)	3500lb (1588kg)
No. 4 (11mm)	4200lb (1905kg)

Kernmantel (Sheath and Core or Jacketed Core)

The construction of this rope consists of an outer braided sheath with an inner core [b]. The design of the inner core varies with different manufacturers. Rope of this type should conform to the UIAA specification and it is recommended that 11mm with a minimum breaking strain of 5000lb (2268kg) be used for climbing.

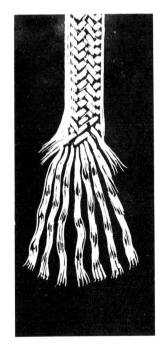

[b]

Table of Rope Size and Strength

Size	Breaking Load
9mm	3200lb (1452kg)
11mm	5000lb (2268kg)

Choosing a Rope

It is common now to climb with a 150ft (45m) rope. Double ropes are quite often used on hard rock climbs and they are usually two separate 9mm kernmantel ropes or two No. 3 hawser-laid ropes. It is usual for these ropes to be of different colours.

Some 300 ft/90 m ropes are bi-coloured, e.g. half-red, half-white.

Hawser-laid rope is usually cheaper to buy than kernmantel, but the latter has the advantage of smoother handling and less friction. When learning to climb or for small outcrop climbing, hawser-laid rope is quite satisfactory and shouldn't be discarded just because it is no longer fashionable.

Carrying the Rope

There are many ways of carrying a rope but the simplest way is in the form of a coil over the shoulder.

To form the coil, take the rope in the left hand (assuming you are right-handed) and with the right hand, form loops in the left hand, first rolling the rope between the thumb and first finger to remove kinks or twists.

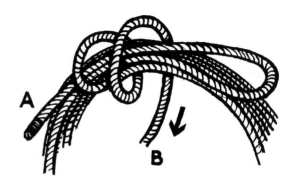

To secure the coil, fold end 'A' back to make a loop.

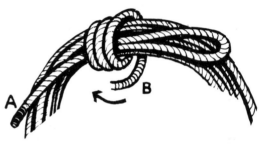

Now use the other end 'B' to whip about five tight turns around the coils, working back towards the loop.

Pass the end 'B' through the loop and pull the other end 'A' to tighten.

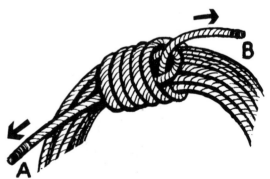

Care of the Rope

The ends of the rope should be sealed with a hot knife or tape to prevent unravelling.

The middle can be marked with a plastic electrical tape or similar. DO NOT USE PAINT OR DYE.

Examine after use for cuts or damage and discard any doubtful rope. THROW IT AWAY after a long leader fall.

Ropes should be stored in a dark, cool, dry place. After being used for sea-cliff climbing or when covered in mud and grit they should be washed in clean water or with mild soap-flakes and dried uncoiled.

Avoid treading on the rope as this forces grit into it and will cause damage.

Do not store rope near radiators or other heat sources.

Do not use a climbing-rope to tow a car.

KARABINERS ('KRABS', SNAPLINKS, MOUSQUETONS, CARABINERS)

'Karabiner' is the name given to a metal link with a spring-loaded gate on one side [a]. It is an essential part of the climber's equipment. There are many makes, shapes and sizes of karabiner currently available.

Most karabiners are now made from specialist aluminium alloys with tensile steels used for springs and rivets. The cross-section of the metal used varies from a 'round' bar to a 'tee' section.

It is common practice to use a UIAA-approved screwgate karabiner [b] (minimum breaking strain of 2500kg) for attaching the rope to the climber when using descendeurs, for belaying and when abseiling. There is much to commend this practice as many accidents have occurred in those instances where non-screwgate karabiners were used.

Some climbers advocate the use of two karabiners in opposition [c] in lieu of a screwgate. This is acceptable but increases the number of karabiners required.

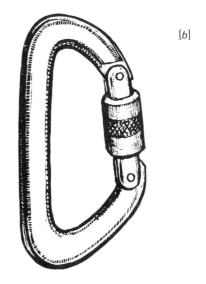

[b]

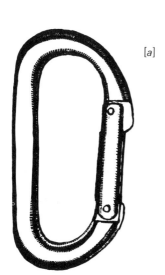

[a]

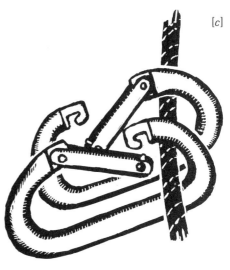

[c]

A Few Hints on Using Karabiners

1. Wash and dry all karabiners after use on sea cliffs.
2. After use check for loose or stiff gates. Oil the gates occasionally wiping excess oil off so that it will not attract dirt.
3. When using 'non-screwgates', ensure that the gates are positioned so that they cannot be opened by rocks or projections.
4. Never use plain karabiners in a chain – they can twist and open.
5. Avoid 'three-way' loading and sideways loading.
6. If a karabiner is dropped down a cliff, it should be discarded, as unseen hairline cracks could be present.

SLINGS

These are made from nylon rope or tape [a]. The length of the sling varies depending on the use. The strongest possible sling should always be used remembering that the introduction of a knot always reduces the strength of the material at that point.

Rope slings can be made by purchasing a length of 11mm (No. 4) rope, cutting it up into suitable lengths (say 10ft or 3m) and joining the ends with a double fisherman's knot.

Tape can be bought as ready-stitched loops [b] or cut to your own length and joined using the tape-knot.

To avoid the danger of nylon over nylon, each sling will require a karabiner.

Care of Slings

Slings should be treated and examined in the same way as a climbing-rope. They should be thrown away at the first sign of wear. Some climbers use a protective sleeve on rope slings to reduce excessive wear.

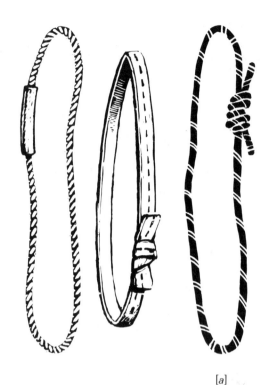

[a]

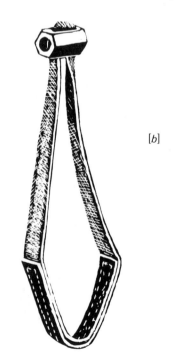

[b]

Other Equipment

Nuts and chocks [a], pitons [b], hammers [c], holsters [d], ascendeurs [e] and descendeurs [f] are all described in later chapters.

[d]

[a]

[e]

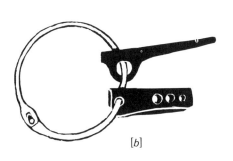

[b]

[c]

[f]

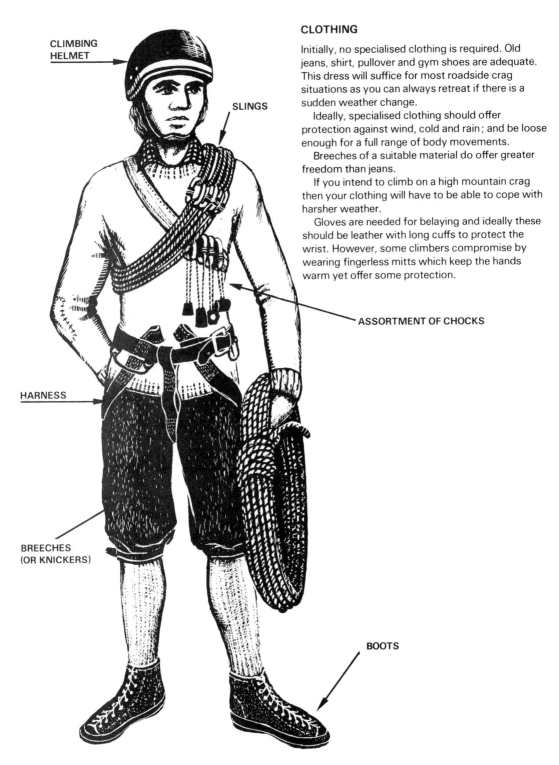

CLIMBING
HELMET

SLINGS

CLOTHING

Initially, no specialised clothing is required. Old jeans, shirt, pullover and gym shoes are adequate. This dress will suffice for most roadside crag situations as you can always retreat if there is a sudden weather change.

Ideally, specialised clothing should offer protection against wind, cold and rain; and be loose enough for a full range of body movements.

Breeches of a suitable material do offer greater freedom than jeans.

If you intend to climb on a high mountain crag then your clothing will have to be able to cope with harsher weather.

Gloves are needed for belaying and ideally these should be leather with long cuffs to protect the wrist. However, some climbers compromise by wearing fingerless mitts which keep the hands warm yet offer some protection.

ASSORTMENT OF CHOCKS

HARNESS

BREECHES
(OR KNICKERS)

BOOTS

BASIC EQUIPMENT REQUIRED TO START CLIMBING

The following list of equipment gives the minimum required by two people to start climbing in a simple way – e.g. outcrop or top-rope climbing.

45 mm No. 4 hawser-laid rope

2 slings No. 4 (as above) – 8 ft/3 m before tying – for belaying and abseiling

2 slings Troll Super blue-stitched tape 8 ft (3 m) long for belaying and abseiling

2 short slings (4 ft/1 m) of rope or tape for extending wired chockstones

4 UIAA-approved 2500 kg screwgate karabiners

6 UIAA-approved alloy non-screwgate karabiners

6 assorted chockstones on wire and rope

2 climbing helmets

2 climbing belts

The prudent climber will also carry in his pockets a whistle, a sharp pen-knife, and two small prusik loops.

Chapter Two: Learning to Climb

WHERE TO LEARN

Bouldering

One of the best introductions you can have to rock-climbing is to spend a few hours scrambling and just moving about on easy-angled practice boulders (opposite).

This time will not be wasted as it will teach you the correct placing of the feet, develop your co-ordination and generally tune you up to the movement that you will be using when you actually start roped climbing.

Many climbers unable to travel to a suitable rock-climbing area except at the weekend will usually try to spend some time during the week bouldering. This enables them to remain fit and supple for the sport. They are also able to practise and develop particular skills and techniques.

Climbing-walls

The great increase in the numbers of people rock-climbing, and the demand for practice facilities, have led to the increased use of climbing walls where experienced climbers can develop skills, as in the bouldering situation. It is evident that climbing-walls are being used more than ever to introduce beginners to the sport, and indeed many top rock-climbers today regularly use artificial walls for training.

Most walls are built of bricks and it is usual for bricks to be removed and various projections added in order to simulate a rock face. Some are housed in sports halls, others are attached to gymnasia, schools and commercial developments.

Problems have arisen with some climbing walls, due in many cases to restrictive management policy, wrong location, bad design, and poor choice of materials. However it would be fair to say that these problems can be solved if attention is given to these points at the design stage.

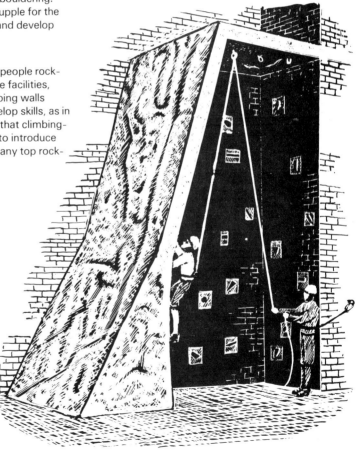

WHAT TO LEARN

Learning to climb rock has been likened to climbing
a ladder placed against a cliff [a]. A few basic
principles are followed; to some people they are
second nature while others have to work at the
skills until they become second nature. Later on,
these principles can be adapted to suit your
climbing-technique.

Three Points of Contact

Initially when learning to climb, it is better to try to
maintain at least three points of contact with the
rock [b] and to move only one hand or foot at a time.

Standing Upright

If you stand upright, the body is in balance, your
weight is directly over the footholds and your feet
are more likely to stay in position [c].

   You will also be able to look down and see where
you are placing your feet. Your body position will be
helped if the heels are kept low; this will counteract
the natural tendency of the beginner to lean into the
rock-face.

[b]

[a]

[c]

[a]

The Position of the Hands

Try to resist the early temptation to reach too high for holds [a]. This destroys the principle of three points of contact and tends to be very tiring on the arms. Let the legs do the work. Ideally, at this stage in your experience, the arms should be used to keep the body in balance.

ALWAYS, AS A MATTER OF PRINCIPLE, TEST ALL HOLDS BEFORE USE. However, if a hold is loose it need not be completely discarded, because it could perhaps be used as a secure hold in another direction. A note of caution: this decision does require some degree of experience.

Thinking Ahead

It is important to look at the next section of the climb in front of you and work out the placing of your hands and feet [b]. Initially, this usually requires some thought, but as you gain in experience, it will become automatic. Starting off a sequence of moves with the correct foot is important as it can be awkward to be 'wrong-footed' halfway through the sequence. If this happens, it usually means reversing the moves back to your original position and starting again.

Practice

Boulders and climbing walls give unique opportunities for the climber to develop technique and to experiment with various combinations of holds in controlled situations [c]. Moves can be repeated over and over until they are perfect. Familiarity with the move enables you to make constructive comments to your partner when he attempts them and vice versa.

[b]

[c]

FEATURES OF A ROCKFACE

When viewed from a distance, a rockface appears to be vertical, smooth and unclimbable. However, closer examination shows that it is perhaps not as steep as first imagined. It is also split by ledges, thin cracks and chimneys. These faults provide the means by which the climber can make progress up the cliff.

The various features on the cliff are worth looking at in detail as they will provide a clue to the type of climbing that you are likely to experience.

Glacis [a]

Rock inclined between the horizontal and 30° is given the name 'glacis' but this is a rather obsolescent term. Because of the low angle the rock can usually be walked up without too much trouble. Care should be taken not to dislodge loose stones that can lie on this type of rock due to its low angle.

Slabs

This name is given to rock at an angle between 30° and 75° [c, opposite]. This probably gives the most common type of rock problem and tends to offer delicate climbing at most degrees of difficulty.

Most easy-angled slabs give excellent training for beginners as they help to develop the technique of balance and the use of various holds. They may form the pitch of a climb or may cover a large area and hold many climbs.

[a]

[b]

Walls

A rock face between 75° and 90° is usually called a wall. Walls tend to give strenuous and delicate climbing, usually with some degree of exposure. The word 'wall' is sometimes used to describe the face of a mountain.

Overhangs [b, opposite]

Short overhangs are usually climbed free. Overhangs which are almost horizontal are called roofs and are usually climbed by artificial techniques.

Climbing overhangs free is strenuous but not necessarily difficult if good holds are available and the correct techniques are used. Generally, it is best to keep the feet on the rock and the body bunched up. However, on some overhangs, it is possible to bridge out and attain a position of balance.

Crack

A fissure in a rock face [d] will vary in width and may be vertical, horizontal or sloping. Some fissures will be very narrow while the wider ones can be climbed by various methods of jamming. Crack climbing is usually safe, as there are numerous possibilities for protection by thread belays and chockstones.

[c]

[d]

[a]

Chimney

When a crack becomes wide enough to accept the body, it is called a chimney [a]. The climbing technique employed depends on the width, and the number and quality of holds available.

Gully

A gully is a cleft in the cliff or mountain side wider than a chimney. Usually these offer easier ways up the rockface and were therefore some of the first rock features to be climbed. As they tend to offer natural drainage, they are often wet and usually contain chockstone and chimney pitches.

Corner

This is a place where two rock walls meet more or less at right-angles [b] in a manner similar to a book opening up. This type of rock feature is common in

[b]

rock climbing and if a crack is present, the corner may be climbed by jamming or laybacking. When no crack is present, the corner is usually tackled by bridging.

Groove

When two walls meet at an angle, it is usually called a groove. If the angle is wide it is usually known as a shallow groove. If it is a right-angle, the term 'corner' applies and if the angle is acute, the name 'vee groove' may be used. In practice, the terms groove and corner are applied loosely and are more or less interchangeable. A groove generally has narrower side walls than a corner.

Rib

A short, blunt rock ridge protruding from the rock face usually with short sides [c].

Arête

A much sharper formation than a rib; the angle of an arete can be anything from horizontal to vertical.

Stance

The name given to the place at the top of a pitch where a climber stands or sits in reasonable comfort and manages the rope [d]. A stance has anchor points preferably close at hand. Comfort (a relative term) is important when taking a stance as the climber is likely to be there for some time whilst belayed. He cannot manage the rope with 100 per cent concentration if he is poorly balanced or sitting in a painful position. Even so, adequate stances can be taken in awkward positions.

[c]

[d]

[a]

[b]

[c]

TYPES OF ROCK

Gritstone, limestone and sandstone are three types of sedimentary rock which were originally laid down as beds and now make up many of the short, steep outcrops used by climbers in Great Britain.

Because of the horizontal bedding and the nature of the rock together with weather erosion, gritstone [a] and sandstone [b] tend to provide rounded rock with rough cracks and overhangs. Sandstone being somewhat softer usually results in the holds being more rounded.

Limestone [c] is usually smoother and provides little pocket holds and thin cracks. However, it is sometimes fractured and not always sound. As well as outcrop climbing, it provides some of the major sea cliff and large roof climbing in Britain. In the Alps, it forms much of the Bernese and Eastern Alpine ranges.

[a]

[b]

[c]

Igneous rock provides the climber with granite, rhyolite and gabbro, probably some of the best rock to climb. Gabbro [a], the principle rock of the Cuillins on the Isle of Skye, off the west coast of Scotland, is very rough, providing walls and large slabs. Granite [b] is generally very firm, giving large blocks with long cracks. The walls and faces of the Yosemite Valley, California are probably some of the finest examples of granite climbing anywhere in the world. Good granite is also found in the French Alps and elsewhere around the world. Rhyolite [c] can provide sound rock with spikes, cracks and slabs. When covered with lichen, it becomes very greasy when wet. Most of the rock in North Wales, and in the Lake District of north west England is of the rhyolite type.

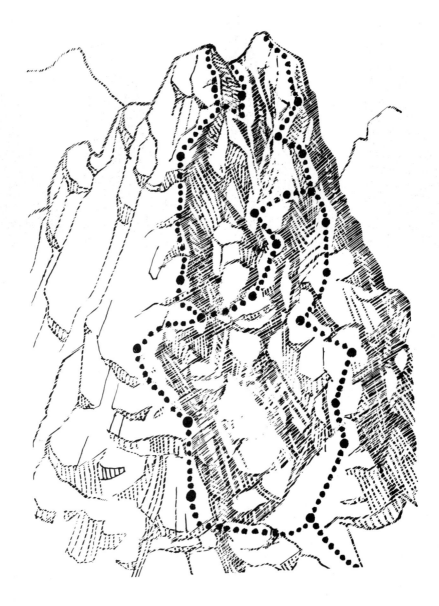

THE ROCK CLIMB ITSELF

Climbers split a rockface into sections between the various ledges or stances and these are called 'pitches'. They vary in length from 40–50 ft (15 m) to well over 100 ft (35 m) in some instances. The diagram shows some fictitious routes divided into pitches. Climbs are usually named and graded for degree of technical difficulty by the first party to climb the route.

Most of the relevant information on the route, such as its location, length, number of pitches, description, is given in a guide book published for the particular crag or area. Details of the grading system used is given later in this book.

To understand the mechanics of roped climbing, it will help if you understand the climbing sequence and the climbing calls.

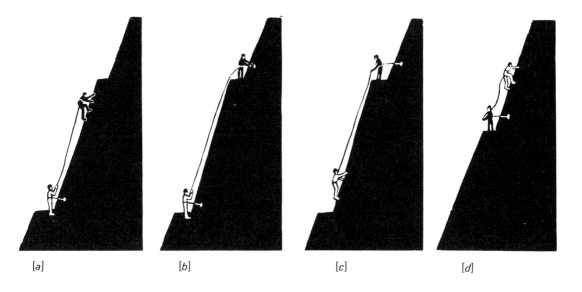

[a] [b] [c] [d]

THE CLIMBING SEQUENCE

Initially, we will look at the sequence in general
terms and then in detail, step by step, later in the
book. When climbing a route, a set pattern of
movements is nearly always followed. It is usually
faster to climb in a party of two with three being the
maximum. Any more on the rope results in a very
long laborious climb, and the waste of a lot of time
at stances.

When the climbing party have located the start of
the climb, the first thing they do is to uncoil the rope
and tie on. The lead climber is sometimes referred
to as No. 1, the second No. 2 and so on.

Depending on a variety of factors, the second
may belay at the foot of the climb [a]. This is usually
done if there is steep ground below the foot of the
climb, if the climb is on a sea cliff, or if the leader
intends to use runners. The leader will then climb
the first pitch of the route. When he reaches a
suitable stance, he will stop to find a suitable rock
anchor and belay there [b].

When the ropework has been completed and the
various calls made, the second can start climbing
[c]. On reaching the stance, he can do one of two
things. He either climbs past No. 1 and continues up
the next pitch (leading through) [d] or he can belay at
the stance and let the original leader continue the
climb by leading the next pitch.

This whole process is repeated for each pitch
until the climb is completed.

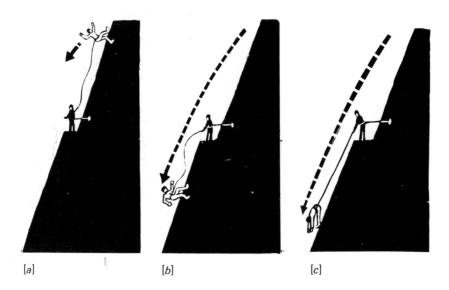

[a]   [b]   [c]

RUNNING BELAYS

It should be obvious from the sequence described
so far, that the second on the rope is well protected
and, as long as the leader is doing his job
conscientiously, shouldn't fall more than a few feet
if he comes off the rock.

A leader fall is potentially a more serious situation
[a]. For example if the leader fell when he was 10ft
(3m) above the second belayed at the first stance,
then he would fall at least 20ft (6m).

Depending on the belay method used, it could
require considerable skill to hold or stop such a fall
[b and c].

However, the leader can safeguard himself by
placing a 'runner' and forming a 'running belay' [d].
The climbing rope is then clipped into this runner
and should the leader fall, then he will only fall twice
the distance he is above that runner, as long as it
stays in position. This is where the skill of the leader
becomes important. Thus the leader can proceed up
the pitch, placing runners when the situation
requires it. The force exerted on the second should
the leader fall will be in an upward direction [e]; a
much easier force to hold as it is almost in the form
of a counterweight. However, the second's belay
must be capable of withstanding this upward force.

[d]   [e]

CLIMBING CALLS

There must obviously be communication between the climbers on a rope. The calls listed on the next few pages are in general use with variations in the actual words used. This does not matter as long as the climbing partners understand their own system of calls.

Try not to combine calls as this can cause confusion. It is often necessary really to shout the calls, especially on a windy day.

When climbing on a local outcrop when there are many other 'ropes' climbing side by side, it is a good idea to prefix your calls with your companion's name. This avoids the embarrassing situation of your second arriving at your stance before you have belayed, because he has acted upon the calls of an adjacent climbing party.

CALL	GIVEN BY	MEANING
'Taking in' 	LEADER	The leader has arrived at the stance, formed the belay and is taking in the slack rope between himself and the second. At this stage the second is still belayed.
'That's me 	SECOND	Used by the second to confirm that the rope is tight between himself and the leader and that it is not caught anywhere.
'Climb when you're ready' 	LEADER	Indicates that the leader is prepared for the second to start climbing. The second, on hearing this call, can start to untie his belay. The slack rope will be taken up by the leader. However the second does not actually start climbing yet. He waits till the next two calls have been given.

CALL	GIVEN BY	MEANING
'Climbing' 	SECOND	Called by the second to the leader, indicating that he is ready to start climbing.
'O.K.' 	LEADER	The final go-ahead by the leader for the second to commence climbing.
'Slack' 	CLIMBER	Used by the climber when he requires a little rope, perhaps to step down a few moves before having a further try.

CALL	GIVEN BY	MEANING
'Take-in'	CLIMBER	Request by the climber for the slack rope to be taken in by the belayer. Try to avoid the phrase 'Take in slack'. It combines two opposite requests and if misheard could lead to trouble in extreme situations.
'Tight' or 'Tension'	CLIMBER	Indicates that the climber requires help from the rope (i.e. he may be about to fall off). The amount of tension depends on the circumstances.
'Runner on'	CLIMBER	Used by the climber to belayer to indicate that he has placed a running belay. The belayer then prepares himself for a pull coming in an opposite direction.

Bad Weather Communication

In extremely bad weather conditions when even shouted calls would not be heard, climbers often work out their own system of tugs on the rope as a means of communication [a].

This system has to be used with caution. It is not unknown for the second to arrive at the stance thinking that the tugs on the rope were an indication to start climbing when in reality the leader was trying to free the rope which had jammed in a crack!

'Below' ('Rock')

As more and more people are climbing, it is often rare to be in the situation where you are the only rope on the crag. It is therefore very important to make sure that you do not dislodge any stones or drop any equipment down the cliff that could injure or even kill somebody.

If you do accidently drop or dislodge something, then it is standard practice to shout 'BELOW', in a very loud voice [b].

The question everyone asks is, 'What do you do when you hear the call?' Do you look up and then move, hoping the object doesn't hit you in the face? Or do you just stay where you are or even move unwittingly into the line of stone fall? Personally, I prefer not to look up, but to look for cover towards the rock face.

The call is also used when throwing the end of a rope down to the foot of a short cliff [c]. 'Rope below' will let others know a rope is coming and they can take evasive action.

Don't make a habit of throwing coiled ropes down a cliff – it doesn't do them any good.

[a]

[c]

[b]

CLIMBING DOWN

This is an aspect of climbing that is generally ignored, but it is a technique that is well worth developing. As your climbing ability increases, there will be many occasions when for various reasons you may have to reverse a few moves.

The procedure for descending a route as a roped party is similar to that of the ascent except that the more experienced climber goes last. The onus is on the first climber descending the route to place runners to protect the last person down. As runner placing is a technique usually carried out by the leader, this opportunity will be good experience for the second.

Which way to face when climbing down can be a problem. On easy ground it is better to face out and use pressure holds for the hands [b]. Obviously, it is easier to see where you are going.

[b]

[a]

TOP ROPING

When you start climbing, you may not be fortunate enough to meet up with an experienced leader, so your first climbs could be safeguarded by means of a top rope. In many areas there are small outcrops of rock perhaps 30–40 ft (10–12 m) high that are ideally suited for top roping.

On some outcrops, such as sandstone edges, it is possible to use an anchor point such as a substantial tree at the top of the climb [a]. By the use of a sling and karabiner it is possible to hold the climber from the bottom of the cliff. This is especially useful when you are learning to climb and want to watch your partner to correct faults or offer advice or whatever.

If there are no obvious anchor points close to the edge of the cliff, then you will have to arrange the belay so that you are at the top of the cliff and can throw the spare end of the rope down.

As the going gets more difficult, it will be necessary to face in and stand well away from the rock to see where you intend to place your hands and feet [a]. Remember to keep the hands low.

STUDY OF LEADERS

The beginner to rock climbing can learn a tremendous amount just by watching a leader climb [b]. Try to remember the sequence of moves, how, why and where he places the protection. Having an enquiring mind and never taking anything for granted will quickly increase your knowledge and enable you to develop your own leading ability.

[a]

[b]

Chapter Three: Climbing Techniques

Climbing technique will vary with the type of hand and foot hold available, the type of rock features being climbed and finally, the state of the rock. It could be firm or loose, wet or dry. Some rock such as limestone becomes extremely slippery when wet.

In this chapter we will look at the various types of holds encountered and how to use them, then examine rock features and the techniques used to climb them.

HAND-HOLDS

Holds vary in size and shape but the most important consideration is the way they are used. Some are extremely small whilst others are very large and reassuring and can be grasped with the whole hand. These are usually referred to as 'jug handles', (abbreviated to 'jugs'), 'thank-God holds', or even 'buckets'.

We will now look at holds in detail.

Flat Holds [a]
The flat of the hand is usually placed close to the edge of the hold so that the fingers can explore for small irregularities in the rock that will improve the grip.

Finger Holds [b]
When the hold is very small it usually helps to raise the knuckles so that just the ends of the fingers rest on the hold.

Incut Holds [c]
This is the type of hold that all climbers are thankful for at some time. They can be used for strenuous pull-ups but in doing this there is a tendency to waste energy on them.

Pressure Holds [d]
As the name implies, this hold is used by pressing down with the heel of the hand, usually on to a sloping surface. The fingers usually point downwards helping to support the hand. Quite often the pressure hold is turned into a 'push up' hold as the body moves upwards to complete a sequence.

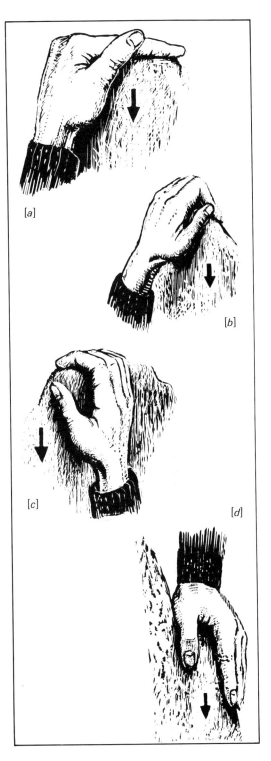

[a]

[b]

[c]

[d]

Mantelshelf

This technique is used to gain a ledge when there are no useful holds immediately above or below the ledge. The mantelshelf consists basically of four movements.

a. Hands are placed on the edge of the ledge.
b. The feet are positioned as high as possible.
c. With a co-ordinated movement, the body is moved upwards so that the arms are in the straight pressure-hold position.

d. A sideways movement is made to place a foot on the ledge. It is then a question of standing up on the ledge.

The secret of mantelshelfing, especially above the head, is to place the feet as high as possible and to make sure that the upward body movement is strong and continuous. Try if possible to avoid using the knee when landing on the ledge. If the ledge is narrow, you may be unable to gain your feet.

[a]

[b]

[c]

[d]

Pinch Grip

This involves pinching a protrusion of rock with the fingers. Its effectiveness depends largely on the strength of the fingers [a].

Sometimes the fingers are inserted into a crack and pull against the thumb which pushes on a knob of rock [b].

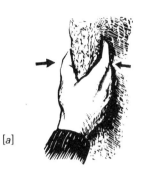

[a]

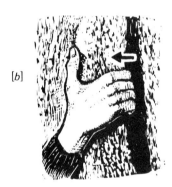

[b]

Undercut Holds

The underside or the bottom edge of a flake can provide a really effective hold. However, care should be taken to test the hold beforehand as considerable leverage could be exerted on a long flake, resulting in its fracture.

Side Pull

Up to now we have considered most holds as being horizontal. Whilst this is probably the ideal, side holds can be used effectively as opposition holds.

Layback

This is basically another opposition hold. The hands grasp the edge of the crack whilst both feet on the wall push in opposition. It is important not to allow the hands to get too far from the feet. Any footholds that can be used for the feet simplify the climbing.

A steady rhythmic movement is preferable to a series of quick, strenuous dashes. This is the type of movement that it pays to practice beforehand on boulders or climbing walls.

NARROW CRACKS

As we have seen in Chapter Two, cracks vary in width from those that are very narrow, to those that will accept the whole body.

Finger Jamming

In narrow cracks the fingers can be 'jammed' by a twisting action of the wrist and palm, i.e. with the thumb pointing downwards. The grip of the fingers can be increased by pushing in opposition on the edge of the crack with the thumb.

Hand Jamming

This technique was developed and used with great effect by Joe Brown, the world-famous English climber. It is formed by bringing the thumb diagonally across the palm thus increasing the thickness of the palm.

A good hand jam gives a feeling of security and enables you to stand well out from the rock face to find good footholds.

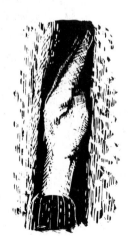

Fist Jamming

As the width of a crack increases it may be necessary to clench the hand into a fist and insert it across the crack. With this hold, it is easier to rely on the fist acting as a 'chock' rather than relying on just muscle strength.

WIDE CRACKS

Arm Jamming

When cracks become about 6 in (150 mm) wide, they are awkward to climb by hand jamming methods. They are then usually tackled by arm jamming, which is basically the technique of opposition pressure and tends to be very strenuous.

The whole of the arm up to the shoulder is pushed into the crack with the shoulder and elbow pressing against one wall whilst the hand is pressed in opposition against the other wall.

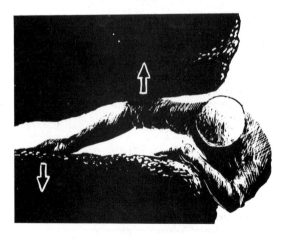

The leg and foot can also be jammed into the crack to help progress, whilst the other hand is also used in opposition on the side of the crack.

Hand Traversing

This can be very tiring and strenuous but the technique to use is to keep the feet high and not to let the arms become extended [a]. A quick rhythmic movement across the traverse will pay dividends.

Foot movements can become complicated but it is usually better to bring one foot up to the other rather than stepping through.

On long traverses, it is important for the leader to use adequate runners to safeguard the second, and himself, against 'penduluming' in the event of a fall.

[a]

CHIMNEYS

Cracks over 15 in (37 cm) wide are usually termed chimneys and are climbed in a variety of ways according to the width [b].

For clarity, ropes have been omitted from this and the subsquent drawing.

Wriggling

This method tends to be very strenuous and awkward. Progress is made by wriggling up a little and then jamming the feet or body whilst you rest and look for further holds. Pressure hand holds are very useful with this type of climbing. It is sometimes possible to position a foot behind you to support yourself whilst the body is moved up.

Starting the chimney facing the correct way is very important but this can be difficult if the climb is new to you. Generally it is better to climb facing the wall with the most holds on it.

[b]

Backing

This is the accepted classic method of climbing chimneys. The feet are placed on one wall and both hands and back on the other wall. This is another example of opposition pressure; the hands and the feet are moved alternately. If the chimney is not quite wide enough it may be necessary to jam the feet or heels and the knees on the opposite wall. You can always tell the climbers who do a lot of backing by the patches on their knees.

Bridging (Straddling)

This method [a] is employed in wide chimneys and consists of placing one hand and foot on each wall and utilising all the holds available. Most of the work is done by the feet. The direction you face depends on factors such as the availability of running belays and your nerve. Psychologically, it is easier to face into a chimney than to face out.

FOOTHOLDS

Most of the handholds already described can also be used as footholds. Develop confidence in using your legs and feet and let them do the work. The thigh muscles are probably the strongest muscles in the body, so it makes sense to use them.

The type of footwear being used will usually determine how the footholds are used. With stiff-soled climbing boots the really small holds can be used [b]. Remember to keep the heels low, stand away from the rock and let the weight come on the feet.

[b]

[a]

Rock boots usually rely on friction so it pays to place as much of the boot as possible on the hold [a]. The technique of using the side of the more flexible boots on small holds is worth developing [b].

Sometimes the technique of knee-jamming is used. Care should be taken – some climbers have had to be rescued because they have been unable to unjam their knees!

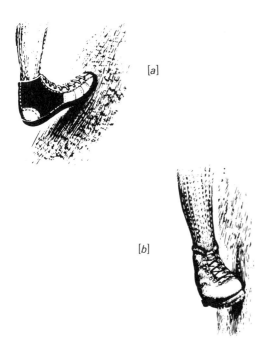

[a]

[b]

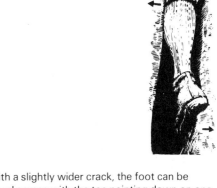

With a slightly wider crack, the foot can be jammed across with the toe pointing down on one side with the heel pressed against the other wall.

Narrow cracks are probably easier to foot-jam using rock boots.

The toe of the boot is inserted into the crack by twisting it sideways and then straightening it. Problems seem to occur when climbers try to pull the foot straight out rather than reversing the sequence.

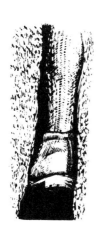

COMBINED HOLDS

Most of the time whilst you are climbing, you will be using a combination of the holds already described. The combinations you use will depend to a large extent on your experience and physical ability.

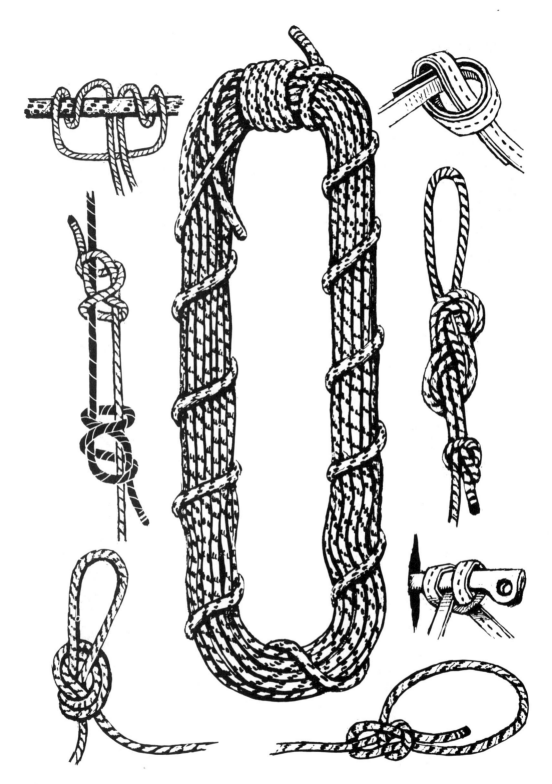

Chapter Four: Knots

Before we consider the subject of knots in detail, it is worth remembering that any knot in a rope will weaken the rope at that point.

Over the years many knots have been used in climbing. Initially it is better to consider just a few simple knots, know when to use them, and more important, be able to tie them quickly and in any circumstances, especially at times when you are tired, wet or cold.

THE BOWLINE

This is the traditional knot for attaching the climbing rope to the climber. Care must be taken when tying knots in nylon rope as they tend to work loose. To prevent this happening, always leave sufficient rope after tying the main knot to tie a stopper knot (e.g. a thumb knot, or two half-hitches).

THE DOUBLE LOOP BOWLINE

Some climbers advocate the use of this version of the bowline knot as they consider that it holds its shape better under load.

FIGURE-OF-EIGHT KNOT

This knot has much to offer the climber. Once learned, it is simple to tie and can be undone easily even after being subjected to considerable load.

The figure-of-eight can be tied in the end of the rope or it can be tied in the middle to be used as a tie-on for a third climber on the rope [a,b,c,d].

An alternative method of tying the knot in the end of the rope is shown [e,f]. A figure-of-eight knot is tied in a single length of rope. The knot construction is then followed with the end of the rope until the complete knot is finished.

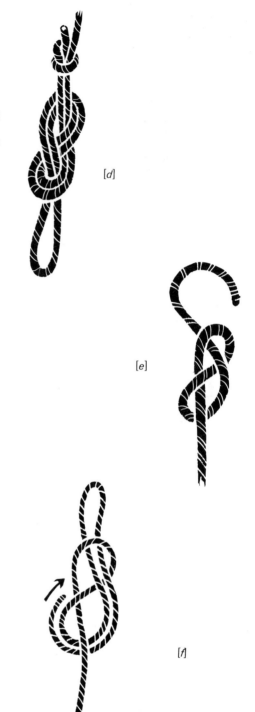

[d]

[a]

[b]

[e]

[c]

[f]

54

STOPPER KNOTS

Overhand or Thumb Knot
This is the simplest stopper knot.

Two Half Hitches
Another common method of securing a main knot.

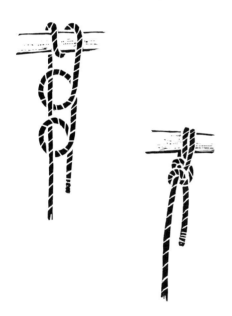

OVERHAND KNOT

This is a simple knot, but having the drawback of being very difficult to untie after subjection to excessive load.

DOUBLE FISHERMAN'S or GRAPEVINE KNOT

This is a very useful knot for joining two ropes of equal thickness. When used for rope slings, it is usual to leave long ends free so that they can be taped down. This prevents the knot working loose and slings from catching on each other when removing from around the neck.

Half Double Fisherman's
Probably the most effective stopper knot.

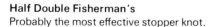

THE SHEETBEND

This knot is often used in place of the fisherman's knot, but it is bulkier and probably more likely to work loose [a]. The double sheetbend is safer than the single variety. This is quite a useful knot for joining up abseil slings as it can be adjusted rather more easily than the fisherman's knot. It is usually recommended for joining two ropes of markedly unequal thickness as it does not distort [b].

TAPE KNOT (RING BEND, OVERHAND BEND or WATER KNOT)

This is the only knot recommended for tying in tape or webbing [a].

An overhand knot is made in one end of the tape and then followed with the other end of the tape to complete the knot [b].

The ends should then be sewn or taped down [c].

If you use tape or webbing for slings, the purchase of stitched loops produced by the manufacturer is recommended [d]. Tests have shown that these have a much higher breaking-strain than a knotted loop.

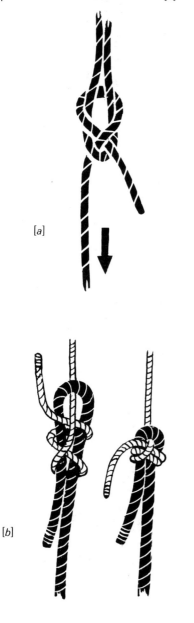

[a]

[b]

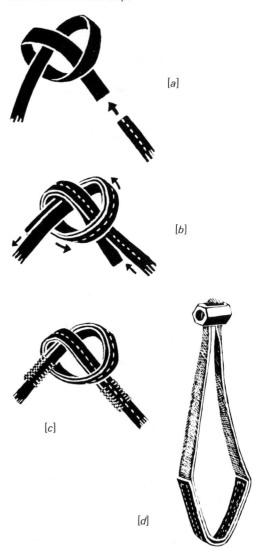

[a]

[b]

[c]

[d]

PRUSIK KNOTS

Prusik knots are sliding friction knots and are used in a variety of climbing situations. Dr Karl Prusik was the first to invent a knot that will slide easily up or down a rope, yet lock when loaded.

The great advantage of the prusik knot is that it is simple to tie and can be attached to the rope with one hand. The easiest way to do this is to roll the knot joining the prusik loop (usually a double fisherman's) around the climbing rope twice and then pull it through itself [a,b].

emergency situations; for instance, hanging from the end of a rope.

[c]

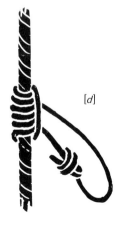

[a]

[b]

Prusik on Worn Rope

The prusik knot can slip on worn or wet ropes. Also, the type of rope, its age and stiffness can affect the efficiency of the knot. However, its grip can be increased by passing the loop three times around the climbing rope [d].

The thickness and type of rope used for the prusik loop is extremely important. Rowland Edwards carried out a series of tests at Plas y Brenin National Mountaineering Centre, North Wales (subsequently published in the magazine *Climber and Rambler* in June 1976), and it would seem that when using an **11mm kernmantel** climbing rope a No. 1 hawser-laid prusik loop will give the best results and can be used with any form of prusik knot.

[d]

The knot should be kept symmetrical and there should be no overlapping of the windings [c], otherwise it could slip when subjected to load. It is a good idea to practise tying this knot in mock

Secondly, a 7 mm kernmantel prusik loop, although not quite as good as No. 1 hawser-laid, will still be trustworthy. The best knot to use with this prusik would appear to be the Klemheist knot.

No. 2 hawser-laid, 5 mm kernmantel and $\frac{1}{2}$ in (12 mm) tape should NOT be used at all for prusiking.

However, this would not exclude them from being used in an emergency situation if these were the only materials available. Care would have to be taken to protect them from being subjected to shock loading.

Bachmann Knot

This knot was introduced in the 1950s and is an improvement on the standard prusik knot. The incorporation of a karabiner provides a useful handhold, which is helpful in moving the knot. The degree of friction is controlled by the number of turns around the back bar of the karabiner and the climbing rope. The knot is recommended for use on wet or icy ropes.

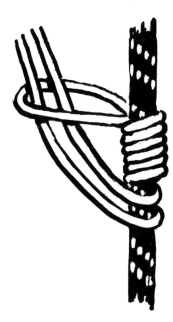

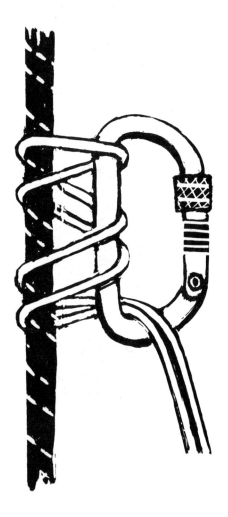

Klemheist Knot

The amount of friction can be controlled by increasing or decreasing the number of turns around the climbing rope. The knot is less liable to jam and easier to loosen than the simple prusik.

It is recommended that with No. 2 hawser-laid rope considerable slip can occur at the knot. It would appear that no slip occurs at the knot with 5 mm kernmantel with the result that the loop usually breaks at the knot. For similar reasons $\frac{1}{2}$ in (12 mm) tape should be avoided.

CLOVE HITCH

Amongst other uses, this knot is used for tying off
pitons.

Two half hitches are formed, one on top of the
other. The loops are then put over the piton and
pulled tight.

'In attempting a corner, I slipped and fell ...' (adapted from Edward Whymper's *Scrambles amongst the Alps*, published in 1871)

Chapter Five: Belaying

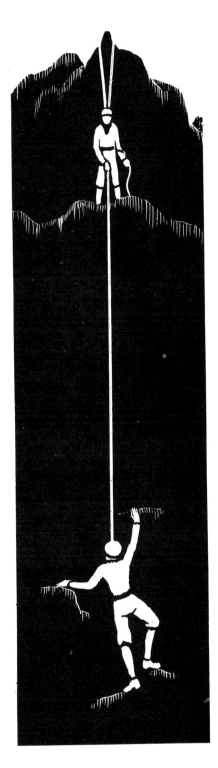

'Belaying' is the general term used to describe the technique used by a climber to safeguard the party from the effects of a fall by one of the group.

A 'static belay' is the method used by the climber to attach himself and the party to firm anchor points.

A 'dynamic belay' is the way the rope is handled when paying out or taking in, at the stance.

Both static and dynamic belaying are the corner stones of 'safe' climbing. Following the tragic accident to Whymper's party after the first ascent of the Matterhorn (1865) there have been numerous detailed studies on belaying techniques.

In this chapter we shall look at selecting anchor points, various static belays, dynamic belays and mechanical belaying devices.

SELECTING THE ANCHOR

It is important to select the anchor point or points with great care, remembering that they could be subjected to considerable force and that your life and the lives of others could be dependent upon them.

Treat each stance and belay as a new situation. Not many are perfect but with the application of a few basic rules they can be made secure.

ALWAYS CHOOSE AN ANCHOR OR ANCHOR POINTS THAT WILL PLACE YOU IN LINE WITH THE EXPECTED DIRECTION OF PULL as illustrated.

If you are not in line you will certainly be pulled into line if the leader falls. In the resulting confusion, seconds have been known to let go of the rope. The leader usually disapproves of this course of action!

SPIKE BELAY

This is the most common type of anchor point and uses any protrusion or flake. Ideally, it should be above shoulder height [a]. Don't just accept a spike on face value. Carry out the following procedures:

1. Make sure that it is solid and part of the rock face.
2. Thump it with the 'heel' of your hand to see if it gives a hollow sound [b] – if it does then leave well alone.
3. Feel it for security by pulling in the direction of the anticipated force – BUT DO SO WITH CARE [c].
4. To minimise the lever effect on the flake, the belay rope or sling should be placed as low as possible [d]. Tape slings lend themselves to use on flakes as they tend to stay in position.

[b]

[c]

[a]

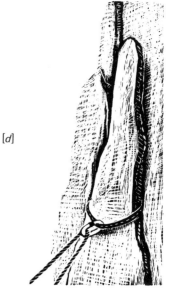

[d]

To form the static belay, place a sling or the rope coming from your waist over the spike [a,b]. Next, with the rope coming from the anchor point, push a loop of rope (called a bight) through your waist tie or karabiner. Tighten the rope between yourself and the anchor point so that there is NO SLACK. When you are in position (ideally at the edge of the cliff so that you can see the second) tie a figure of eight knot back on to the main rope from the anchor [c,d]. Remember to leave a long loop through the knot. Some people tie an overhand knot in this loop to prevent it being pulled through the figure of eight knot [e].

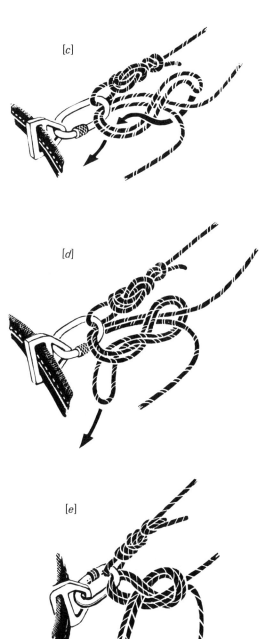

[c]

[d]

[e]

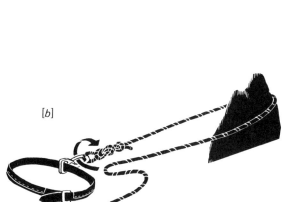

[a]

[b]

To avoid slack rope in the static belay, it sometimes helps to take one pace towards the anchor before tying the knots at the waist. This way you will ensure you are really tight on the anchor when you stand in the correct position [a].

When using the Troll/Whillans harness it is advisable to add a short tape loop at the back of the harness [b], so that the static belay can be attached safely, and there is no danger of the belayer's body being spun violently round in the event of his having to hold a fall.

TREE BELAYS

Trees are acceptable provided they are strong enough, alive and well rooted. As with flakes, the attachment point (i.e. the sling, rope or tape) is best placed as low as possible to limit the lever effect [c].

When using tapes or slings round trees make sure they are long enough [d] so as to avoid three-way loading on the karabiner. Sometimes a sling can be placed above a strong branch to prevent it slipping out of position.

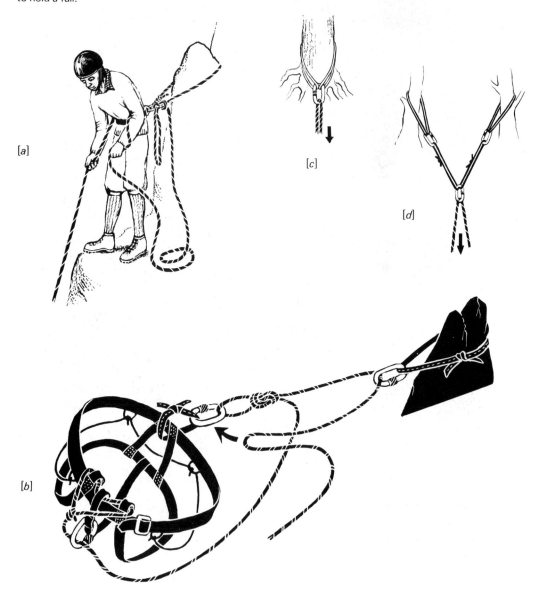

[a]

[c]

[d]

[b]

NATURAL CHOCKSTONE BELAYS

Check that they cannot be pulled out of the crack, especially if the force on the belay is suddenly in a reverse direction e.g. upwards.

If possible, always select at least two anchor points irrespective of the type. Then make sure that they will be equally loaded in the event of a fall. The simplest way to do this is to belay to the first anchor point and adjust the bight of tied-off rope so that it can be clipped into the second anchor. This requires practice to make sure the bight of rope is the correct length.

NATURAL THREAD BELAYS

Generally this is the best type of anchor and as the name implies, the belay is made by threading the main rope or a sling through a hole in the rock or where two *large* rock masses are touching [a].

When available, the thread belay should be used in preference to any other as it will usually take a force in any direction.

Generally it is better to use slings for natural thread belays. This simplifies the procedure; to belay safely with the climbing rope is complicated and uses a considerable amount of rope [b,c,d].

If you do use the climbing rope, the main points to watch are:

1. That you cannot be pulled on to the anchor if you are unable to hold a fall.
2. That the live rope is tied off separately, thus preventing it from undoing the waist tie knot.

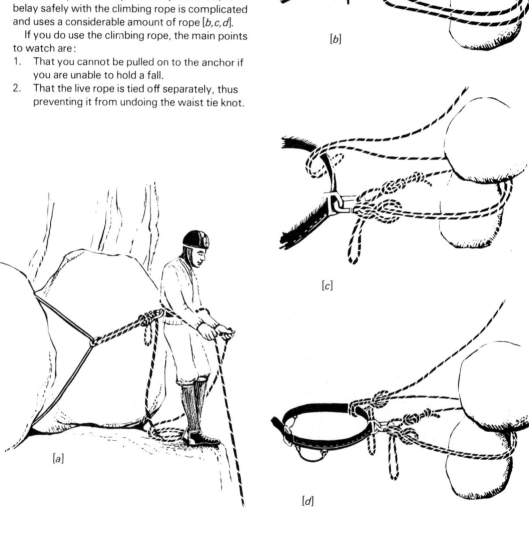

[b]

[c]

[a]

[d]

NUT, CHOCK AND PITON BELAYS

The actual placing of these has been dealt with in the relevant chapters. Generally speaking, nuts and chocks should not be used as *main* anchor points unless there is nothing else available. However, some climbers would argue against this advice.

As mentioned elsewhere, pitons have never found full favour in Britain, but most climbers would accept their use as anchor points for belaying. In the USA and on the Continent of Europe, different climbing conditions have resulted in a different ethical approach.

In some situations, the position of anchor points will dictate that the belayer adopts a sitting position [a]. As long as it is possible to brace the legs, this is a very effective position. It can be uncomfortable if you are sitting in a pool of water.

Another method of equally loading two anchor points is to use a connecting sling [b]. It is important that the sling is twisted as illustrated to ensure that if one anchor point fails, then the belayer will still be attached to the remaining anchor. An alternative method equally loading three anchor points is also shown [c].

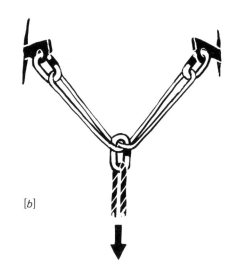

[b]

[a]

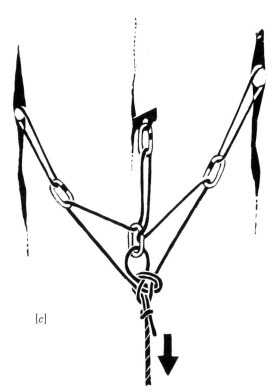

[c]

DYNAMIC BELAY

After the leader has arrived at the stance, selected the anchor points and formed the static belay, he is almost ready for the second to start climbing. The way he controls the rope and the position he adopts is generally referred to as the dynamic belay.

This method, with variations, is more or less the standard procedure used in Britain. Basically the belayer is positioned between the anchor points and the climber and thus absorbs some of the force in the event of a fall. This places less strain on the anchor points but does require a certain amount of skill to perform the operation with ease.

Method

After the belayer has given the call 'taking in', and the second has replied with 'that's me', the belayer places the 'live' rope over his head and around his waist so that it is *above* the belt, harness or waist tie. Make sure that the waist karabiner is turned over so that the gate (better to use a screwgate karabiner) cannot be opened by the rope passing over it.

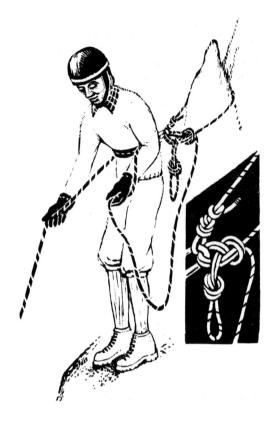

The rope from the climber is, as we have mentioned, called the live rope. The leg and hip on this side should be slightly forward, the other knee slightly flexed, and the legs apart to provide a stable platform.

A turn round the forearm of the other hand, from inside the elbow across the top of the forearm, will give the required extra friction. Gloves, preferably made of leather, with long cuffs, should be worn, and sleeves rolled down, to protect the hands, wrists, and forearms from friction burns.

With a sitting belay, some people advocate the placing of the live rope *below* the static belay rope as it is argued that the fall force if it occurs will be taken on the hips rather than the waist.

This is a valid point but there is a danger that the rope may be pulled down over the hips with resulting problems (i.e. the rope may not be held).

Taking in the Rope

As the second climbs, the rope is 'taken in' so that it is almost taut; thus the second should only fall a foot or so if he comes off the rock. The action of taking in the rope has been said to resemble playing a fish: the rope is taken in as the second moves up, paid out if he steps down to re-examine a series of moves.

The inactive hand is slid back along the inactive rope to the waist, while both ropes are still held in the active hand.

The inactive rope is then gripped and brought forward towards the active hand, at the same time opening the active hand to allow the rope to be pulled through.

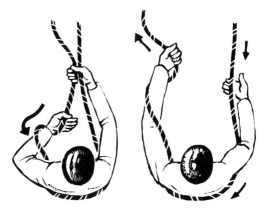

The belayer *always* has hold of the rope. Initially, both ropes are held in the active hand.

Both ropes are gripped once more in the active hand and the whole process repeated.

This action may seem a little strange at first, but you will quickly master it. As it is an essential part of the belay system it is very important to practice beforehand.

As the rope is taken in, develop the habit of placing it on the ledge by your side. Don't let it dangle down the cliff – it would be likely to snag on small spikes or jam in cracks. Also, it might hinder the second while he is climbing.

CHANGING BELAYS

When the leader has brought the second up to the stance, the second has the option of climbing the next pitch or belaying and allowing the leader to continue the climb.

THE SECOND TO CONTINUE AS LEADER

As long as both climbers are competent at leading, then generally this is the quickest way of climbing a route as the delay at each stance is minimal. If the climbing pair are sharing equipment, all that will be necessary is for the new leader to collect sufficient slings, karabiners and possibly some nuts and chocks to protect the next pitch.

While he is sorting out his gear, the new second should make sure that the leader's rope will come off the top of the pile and that it is free of snags. Nobody likes to stop climbing because the second has a tangle of rope (usually referred to as 'knitting').

If the route crosses above the second, then the second must change the direction of the rope round his waist. This must be done in consultation with the leader.

It is worth stressing the point that if the leader were to fall, then the second should always try to absorb the force with the rope across his back and above the anchor ropes. THEREFORE HE MUST FACE OUT FROM THE BELAY. IF HE FACES THE BELAY THE STRAIN WILL COME FROM BEHIND HIM, AND THE ROPE COULD BE WRENCHED OUT OF HIS HANDS.

THE SECOND TO BELAY

The second always belays himself and is still safeguarded by the leader until this is completed. This ensures that both climbers are safe during the change over.

More often than not, the second will use the same anchor points as the leader. This is acceptable but to ensure that the ropes do not tangle it is important that the rope from the second to the anchor goes *underneath* the leader's static belay, as illustrated.

Paying Out the Rope

When the leader is climbing, the second will be paying out the rope in a reverse manner to that used for taking in the rope.

Both ropes are held in the inactive hand; the active hand is then drawn back to the waist.

The active hand grips the rope and pushes it forward, at the same time, the inactive hand releases the inactive rope.

Both ropes are held again in the inactive hand and the whole process repeated.

Normally the leader must have sufficient rope to make at least one or two quick moves, so it is essential that the second is paying attention to his progress.

HOLDING A FALL

A leader fall is potentially serious and will impose great strain on the belayer, even if he has selected his anchor points carefully and is concentrating on his leader's progress (or lack of it).

In the event of a fall, the second initially allows the rope to slide through his hands and then tries to apply a gradual braking effect by gripping the rope. This prevents any shock loading on the anchor points and allows the elastic property of the climbing rope to play its full part in absorbing the force.

To assist the braking effect, some climbers advocate bringing both arms or the live arm across the body to increase the friction. The strain of holding a leader fall is considerable and whatever happens you must not let go of the rope even if you are upside down!

You will now appreciate the reasons for wearing gloves and making sure that the arms are covered.

ESCAPING FROM THE BELAY SYSTEM

If a fall happens, the belayer is faced with certain problems. If the climber is conscious and uninjured then it may just be a case of climbing back up to the stance or being lowered to a convenient ledge. If he is hanging clear of the rock face then he could prusik up the rope – if he is carrying prusik devices or loops.

The unconscious climber on the end of a rope, or a climber unable to help himself, presents a very serious problem, especially if he just has the climbing rope tied round his waist. In this situation the belayer must tie off the rope to the climber as quickly as possible. He then escapes from the belay system and proceeds to ease the strain on the climber before he *dies* from the constricting effect of the rope.

If the inactive rope is wound round a leg and under the foot, both hands can then be used.

A prusik loop is attached to the live rope and clipped into the belay karabiner [a]. If the prusik loop is short, it can be clipped into the waistline karabiner.

If a climbing belt is used which relies for fastening on a karabiner rather than on a buckle, then it is suggested that this prusik loop is NOT clipped into the karabiner.

The prusik loop is slid forward until it is taut and the inactive rope released from round the leg to transfer the load to the prusik. To safeguard the situation a figure-of-eight knot is tied into the inactive rope and clipped into the belay. The belayer's waistbelt or harness can then be undone and assistance rendered to the climber.

A fallen climber who is using a sit harness or body harness in this situation is obviously in a much more comfortable position. It also follows that a prudent climber will always carry a couple of prusik loops.

From all the evidence so far, it would seem sense to try and place a good running belay as soon as possible after leaving the stance. As long as the placement is sound and a good-quality karabiner and strong sling are used, the runner will greatly reduce the force on the belayer and anchor points in an emergency. However, remember that the force on the belayer will be in an upward direction.

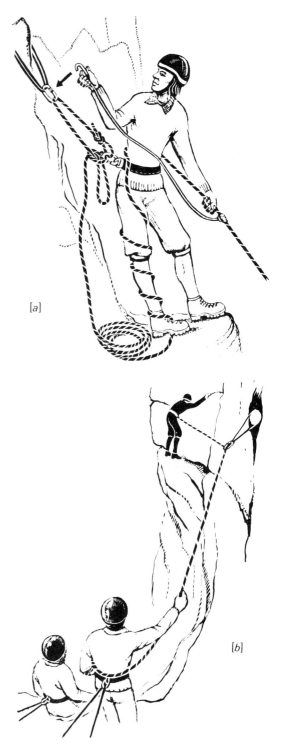

[a]

[b]

THREE CLIMBING ON A ROPE

Up to now, we have considered a rope of two. On some occasions, however, there might be three climbers [b].

In this situation, the leader climbs the first pitch in the normal way. He then brings the second up to the stance.

One of two procedures can then be adopted, the choice depending on the experience of the second man.

Following the first method, the leader can climb the next pitch with the second belaying him; the third person is then brought up to the stance by the second.

Alternatively, all three climbers gather on the first stance; the second then belays the leader up the next pitch – during which time the third person is of course tied on using separate anchor points if available. The second then climbs the pitch, belayed by the leader and also by the third person. The belaying practice is always valuable for the third person and, of course, it is an added safeguard.

The size of the belay stance could of course alter this sequence.

BELAYING DEVICES

During the last few years, there has been a trend towards the use of mechanical belaying devices. Collectively they are known as 'auto belayers' and they are all basically friction devices. The sticht plate is probably the most popular, and so is described in detail.

The Sticht Plate

This very effective device has undergone intensive examination by the UIAA. Basically, it is a round alloy plate $^3/_8$ in (8 mm) thick by some $2^3/_8$ in (59 mm) in diameter. It is available for single 11 mm rope, double 11 mm, or a combination of 11 and 9 mm ropes. The model with a spring is recommended as this prevents the device from locking against the karabiner.

How to Use the Sticht Plate

It is advisable to belay as for a normal dynamic belay. The device is attached to the belt/sit harness or waist tie by a short piece of nylon cord 3–4 in (100 mm) long.

A bight of climbing rope(s) is pushed through the slots in the sticht plate and into a screwgate karabiner(s) which in turn is clipped on to the belt or waist tie.

If a fall occurs, the inactive hand is drawn back immediately and the sticht plate is forced back against the karabiner. The friction developed arrests the fall. There is no need to let reserve rope slide past the belay point as in the normal dynamic belay situation.

The friction developed with the brake can be varied with practice. The angle at which the rope is held during the braking process is important. Do not allow loose clothing or the short nylon cord to be near the brake whilst belaying. These could be dragged into the brake, thereby reducing the dynamic effect.

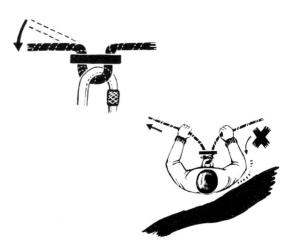

[a]

[b]

The position of the belayer in relation to the cliff face is important when using the sticht plate. There must be freedom for the braking arm.

When the second pitch is commenced the braking arm may have to be changed if the leader's route places him on the other side of the second. The braking effect of the sticht plate can be used in a variety of ways.

1. When the sticht plate is used with one karabiner as illustrated [a] then the braking effect developed will be in the region of 460–490 lb (209–222 kg) force.
2. If the plate is used with two karabiners [b, c], then the braking effect is almost doubled at approx. 880 lb (400 kg) force.
3. When a body belay is incorporated with one karabiner, the braking effect will be approx. 730 lb (331 kg) force.
4. A body belay with two karabiners [d] will produce a braking effect in the region of 1100 lb (499 kg) force.

All the figures quoted will be slightly lower if the rope is wet, as the friction will be reduced.

To a beginner, these figures may not mean a great deal, but they do give some indication of the relative merits of the four methods described.

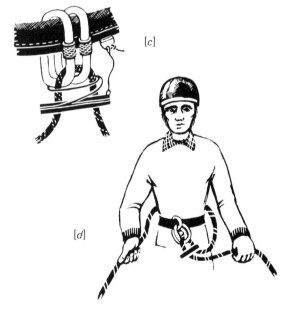

[c]

[d]

As previously mentioned one of the easiest ways to make sure the anchor points are not subjected to high forces, is to use a good running belay as soon as possible [b] – this can reduce the force by as much as 100 per cent.

In some circumstances, when the belay position is not satisfactory for the belay procedure described, then the sticht plate can be attached to a suitable separate anchor point, such as a spike, thread, nut, piton etc [a]. However, the anchor point must be beyond question, as all the force in the event of a fall will come on to this point.

[a]

It is also advisable that the belayer uses separate anchor points and that the plate is low enough for the inactive hand to bring the rope into the braking position.

Finally, the sticht plate is *not* recommended for use with *hawser – laid ropes*.

Belay Practice Machines

The value of dynamic belay practice sessions cannot be over emphasised. At the National Mountaineering Centre in North Wales, the Deputy Director, Roger Orgill, designed a simple device, illustrated opposite, that simulates the effect of a falling climber.

The weight of the concrete block on the device is approx. 140–150 lb (65 kg) and the height of the fall can be varied.

One of the advantages of controlled practice is that other factors can be introduced such as runners, comparison of standing and sitting static belays, and the importance of standing in line. Stress/strain gauges can also be incorporated into the system to check forces imposed on anchor points or any part of the belay.

[b]

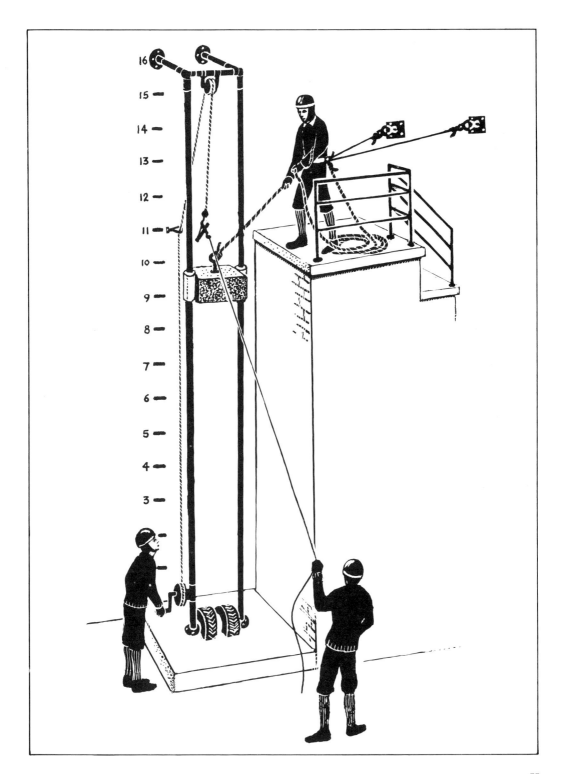

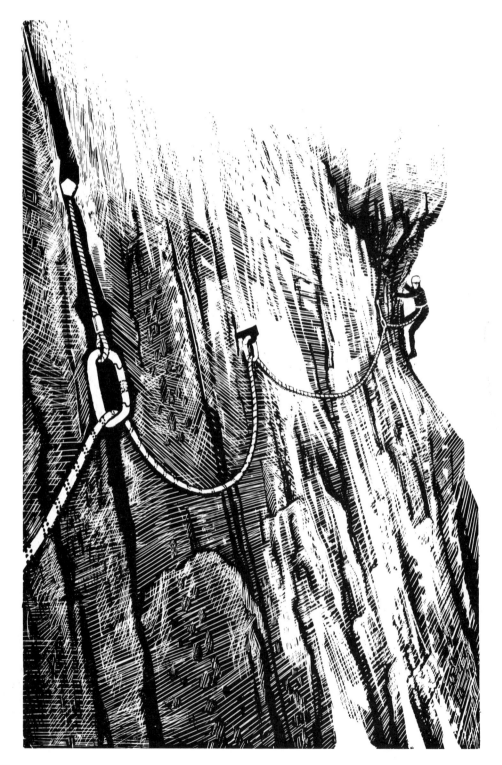

Chapter Six: Pitons and Chocks

Pitons and chocks are artificial aids which can be used in a variety of situations on rock faces, for the following purposes:

1. As anchor points for belaying where no natural anchors are available.
2. As abseil points where there are no suitable natural features.
3. For protection as running belays and for direct aids where the rock face is holdless.

PITONS (PEGS, PINS)

These are metal spikes which can be hammered into existing cracks in the rock face. They have been used sparingly in Britain, whilst in Europe, the US and elsewhere, they have always been used more freely.

In Britain, at least, the use of pitons in rock climbing has always been the subject of endless debate. Generally speaking, on 'free' climbs, they are used for 'points of aid' and for belay situations. Along with bolts, they form the basis for artificial climbing.

As the standard of rock climbing increases, we are seeing the points of aid reduced or eliminated on the majority of free routes. Routes that were considered artificial only a few years ago are now climbed free by an increasing number of climbers.

In the US and elsewhere, the damage to rock caused by the repeated insertion and extraction of hard steel pitons has seen the rapid adoption of nuts and chocks to reduce wear and tear. The result is that a new code of ethics has appeared together with a greater awareness of the environmental damage, such as that illustrated on the right, that can result from the use of pitons.

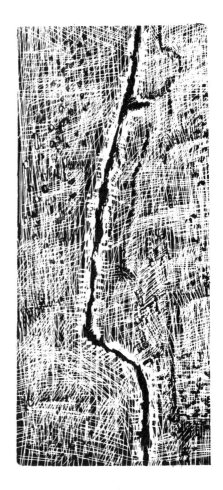

Soft Steel Pitons

Until the 1960s most pitons manufactured in Europe were made from soft, malleable steel which bent on being driven to follow the shape of the crack; consequently they were difficult to extract.

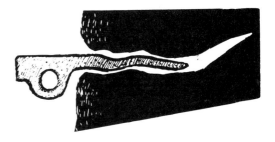

Hard Steel Pitons

At about this time, pitons made from chrome molybdenum steel were starting to be made in the US [a]. The idea of using this material came from John Salathé, a Swiss blacksmith. These pitons proved to be superior in every way and they are now used almost universally. However, it is important that these pitons are examined regularly for cracks developing due to over-use. Their manufacture requires sophisticated techniques and heat treatment to ensure the correct hardness.

Research has indicated that only hard steel pitons have the necessary holding power to withstand a fall in free climbing, and that soft steel pitons are advisable only for artificial climbing.

Pitons have also been made from stainless steel, aluminium alloys and wood. Titanium has also been used – it is strong and light but far too expensive at the moment for commercial use.

PITON SHAPES

Horizontal

The eye is at right angles to the blade and should be the minimum possible distance away from the rock when driven [b]. The latest design usually incorporates an extended anvil to prevent deformation of the eye when driven. The blade is tapered in two directions and sizes vary from short/thin to long/thick.

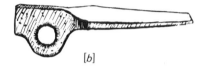

[b]

Vertical

This traditional piton had the eye in line with the blade [c]. Generally it is no longer used in Britain or the US. If a piton is to be used in a vertical crack, it is normal to use one with the eye offset [d]. When a force is applied to this design of piton, the torsional effect greatly adds to its holding properties.

[a]

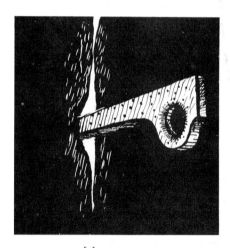

[c]

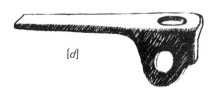

[d]

Angles

The modern angle piton has a 'V' cross section as opposed to the older 'U' section used with traditional soft steel pitons. At one time many of these pitons had welded rings through the eye but they are no longer common in Britain or the US.

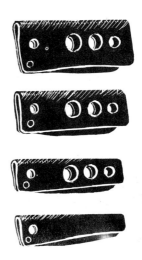

Bongs

When an angle piton is wider than $1\frac{1}{2}$ in (37 mm) it is usually called a 'bong' and is available up to a width of 6 in (150 mm). Because of their size and therefore, weight, bongs are quite often drilled out to reduce weight. They are sometimes made from high-strength aluminium alloy.

Leepers

Named after Ed Leeper from Colorado, leepers have a 'Z' section and excellent holding power when placed correctly. When used in vertical cracks, they are inserted with the eye uppermost. This will ensure that any torsional effect will result in the cutting edges bearing on the rock.

Others

Many other types of piton exist, such as rurps [a], sky hooks [b], bat hooks. These are generally used with advanced rock techniques. A great deal of practice is necessary before one can become proficient and confident in their use.

[a]

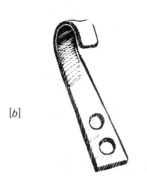

[b]

THE HAMMER

If you look through equipment catalogues you will see many hammers, ranging from the heavyweight models with large striking surfaces, to those that are metal shafted with plastic insulated sleeves, and holes in the head for easy piton removal.

Some lightweight models also have spikes, which are useful for piton removal and for cleaning cracks prior to placing.

The object should be to pick a hammer suited to your needs. It is usually carried in a holster and attached to the belt or harness by means of a length of nylon cord.

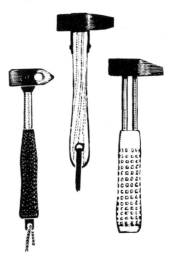

PLACING PITONS

Generally the piton is hand-placed into a crack, if possible for two-thirds of its length, and then driven with the hammer until the head abuts against the rock face. When the piton is being driven a ringing sound steadily increasing in pitch will usually indicate a good placing, whilst a dull sound usually indicates an unsound one. A whining note denotes a blind crack.

Tests have confirmed that the crack in which the piton is placed should run at right angles to the possible direction of force. The plane of the crack will also affect the mechanical advantage of the piton.

Narrowing of the crack above and below the piton will give greater holding power.

When using angle pitons it is important that they are used the correct way up. They have been known to fail when used upside down.

Tied Off Pitons

The occasion may arise when a piton cannot be driven for its full length. The piton must then be 'tied off' to reduce the leverage. This is usually done by using a short loop of 1 in (25 mm) tape and tying a lark's foot or clove hitch.

If there is a danger of the piton karabiner acting as a lever, then the piton should be extended by the additional use of a tape or short sling and karabiner.

REMOVING PITONS

This is usually done by hitting horizontal pitons back and forth as far as possible until they can be taken out. To remove an angle it is usually only necessary to hit them until a small groove is created.

Obviously, it is good policy to avoid dropping pitons whilst taking them out. Apart from the danger of hitting someone, a piton can develop unseen cracks if it falls a good distance – even if one is lucky enough to find it. The most sensible policy would be to abandon that particular piton.

To avoid dropping pitons some climbers clip an old karabiner into the eye of the piton while removing it. This karabiner is attached to the belt or harness by a short nylon cord.

PITON CARRIERS

Pitons are usually carried on a loop of wire or light metal bar, rather like an enlarged key ring. The carrier is attached to a sling, belt or harness.

PRACTICE

On a bad weather day unsuitable for serious climbing, it is worth while spending some time placing and driving pitons, preferably on some out of the way boulders where the scars will not offend anybody. The quality of a good piton placing will depend on three factors:

1.   The soundness of the rock.
2.   The design and material of the piton.
3.   The skill of the person driving the piton.

Try to avoid placing pitons behind detached blocks or flakes.

Sometimes it will be necessary to stack pitons in a crack. This technique can only be acquired by experience.

CHOCKS AND NUTS

Natural chockstones, which are stones or boulders already wedged in cracks, have been used for belaying and the protection of the leader since the earliest days of climbing.

Subsequently, this led to climbers carrying a small selection of pebbles for insertion into cracks. When the need for protection was felt, a short length of line, or even a piece cut off the end of the rope was threaded around one of these pebbles placed in a crack. Thus began the start of the revolution in the use of chocks as we know it today.

One of the earliest examples of the use of this technique in Britain was on the ascent of Central Buttress, Scafell, in 1914.

The use of artificial chockstones has done more than anything to increase the standard of rock climbing. It has also resulted in a greater number of climbers attempting routes of high technical standard.

Basic Types of Chock

The use of engineering nuts with the threads drilled out and sharp edges chamfered off followed the use of pebbles.

This led to the production of specially shaped and designed chocks. Today there is a bewildering range of shapes and sizes available but basically they all work on the principle of wedging. They are also made in a variety of materials ranging from aluminium alloys to brass and plastic.

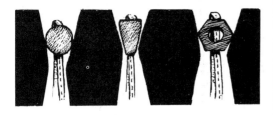

Chocks on Wire

The 'swaged' wire chocks that we know today were first produced in Britain in the late 1960s. Swaging is the technical term for the joint in the wire and is created by hydraulically squeezing a compression sleeve over the lapped joint in the wire. It is said to be the STRONGEST part of the sling. The wire used is usually extra-high-tensile steel, plated to resist corrosion.

Wire chocks have a greater breaking strain than that available using rope or tape. Because of the stiffness of the wire, chocks can sometimes be placed some 6 in (150 mm) or so beyond a climber's normal reach. For this reason, they are sometimes referred to as 'cheating sticks'.

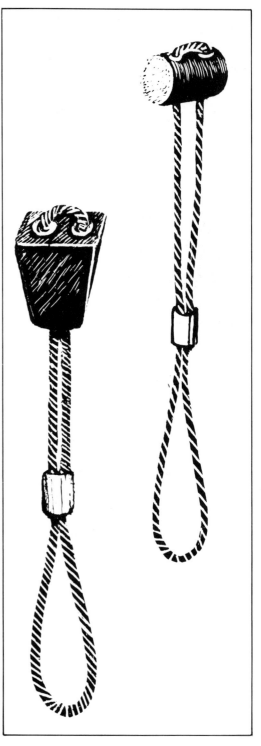

This stiffness, however, can be a disadvantage as it may result in the chock's being displaced by the rope when the leader moves upwards. This can be overcome by lengthening the wire sling by two additional karabiners and a tape or rope sling.

A karabiner must always be used to connect the rope or tape sling to the wire chock. UNDER NO CIRCUMSTANCES SHOULD A 'LARK'S FOOT' BE USED in this situation. Tests have indicated a loss in strength in tape of up to 83 per cent if this fastening is used.

On some wire chocks, plastic sleeves are provided and plastic stoppers to hold the wire together. Climbers sometimes tape the wires together to prevent the chocks tangling through one another.

Chocks on Tape (Webbing) or Rope

Most climbers carry a selection of chocks on rope and tape. From a practical point of view both have their uses. It is sometimes easier to slip tape into a narrow crack below the chock, rather than try and force rope into place.

Both materials should regularly be checked for wear, especially tape in view of its large surface area.

On large chocks, the knot can sometimes be tied so that it will push inside the chock thus presenting a neat and tidy appearance [a].

To reduce the weight of equipment carried on a climb, roped or taped, chocks are sometimes used as runners or anchor slings [b]. If this is done, it is essential that they are used in the illustrated manner [c] to avoid placing undue strain on the sling.

[a]

[b]

[c]

PLACING OF CHOCKS

Generally a chock is placed in a narrowing section of a crack where it will resist a downward force by wedging [a]. Often it can be wedged firmly by a sharp downward pull on the sling to bed the alloy into the grain of the rock.

The use of a hammer is sometimes advocated to seat chocks but this raises the question of ethics as this is almost akin to driving a piton. Most climbers would prefer to see chocks placed in position by hand and left at that.

Some chocks, for instance hexentrics, rely on the wedging effect being created by a torsional force placed on the chock. It is therefore important that the climber understands the mechanics of their placement [b,c,d].

All chocks can be stacked or sandwiched in various ways to fit a given situation and to increase their versatility [e].

Bongs can be used as large chocks [f]. They are normally placed pointing downwards with a tape threaded through the lightening holes or around the entire bong. As they have end taper, they can be used across a wide crack.

[c]

[d]

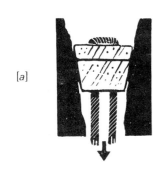

[a]

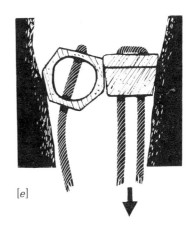

[e]

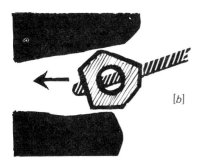

[b]

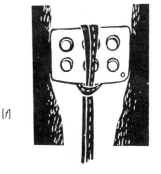

[f]

REMOVAL OF CHOCKS

When placing chocks, the leader should give some consideration to the problems that the second may experience in removing them. Sometimes small chocks can be pushed upwards by using the wire. Any epoxy resin glue between the nut and the wire will prevent the nut slipping down the wire.

CARRYING CHOCKS ON A CLIMB

Most climbers develop their own methods for carrying equipment whilst climbing. Some system is essential to conserve time and energy. Nuts are best carried one to a karabiner and it is usual to 'rack' them in order of size and type so that they come easily to hand.

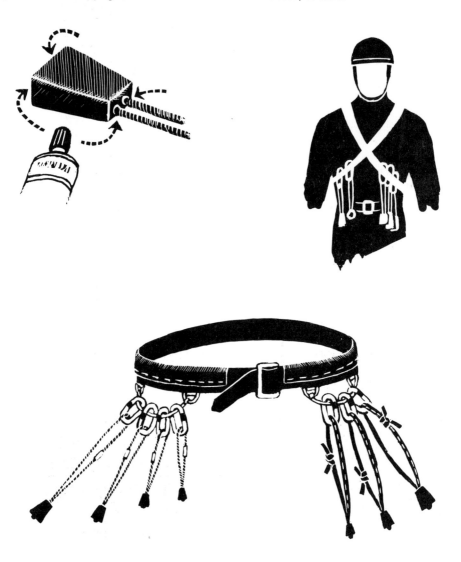

Make sure that you have all karabiner gates opening the same way. It is then easy to remove the chocks without looking at your equipment. It is usual to have the gates opening at the top, towards the body or away, depending on personal preference.

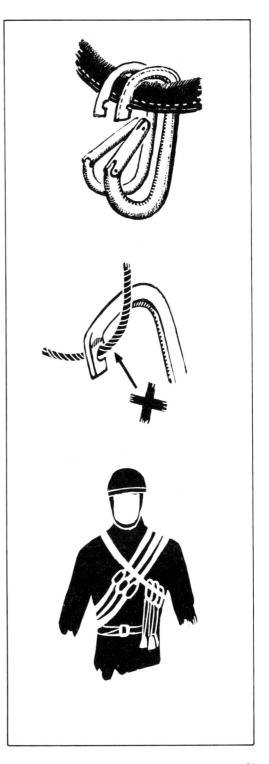

If the carrying cord is too thin, it can catch in the gate of the karabiners.

Long slings (rope or tape) are usually required for belaying and runners. These can be worn bandolier-fashion and placed over the gear-carrying bandolier. The knots can be placed under the arm to prevent snagging.

Short slings are usually carried over the head with the knots at the bottom of the necklace. If the longest is placed over first, followed by the shorter ones, it should be possible to select the correct sling for the situation.

A system of colour coding to indicate the type of chock, wire, tape or rope is used by some climbers.

Chapter Seven: Prusiking and Abseiling

PRUSIKING (JUMARING): THE CLASSIC METHOD

Prusiking (jumaring) is a general term used to describe any method of ascending a climbing rope. The classic method is the simplest [a], and was developed as a system of self-help from crevasses. Three prusik loops are attached to the climbing rope with prusik knots (see pp.57–8). The chest loop should be clipped into the waistline karabiner or it can be tied off at the chest with a suitable knot for additional security.

A 'lark's foot' can be used to secure the boot in the prusik loop [b].

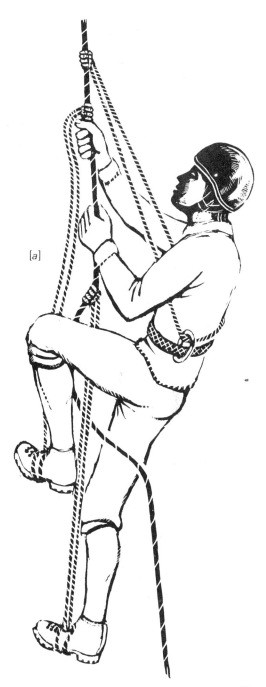

[a]

[b]

When climbing the rope, move only one prusik loop at a time and always make sure that the load is off the knot before attempting to move it. Prusik knots can be awkward to move with gloved hands and the knot incorporating a karabiner is worth considering [a]. The advantage of prusik loops is that they are inexpensive, and, together with karabiners, are normal pieces of climbing equipment.

[a]

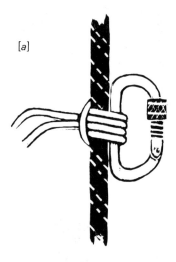

MECHANICAL DEVICES

Prusiking is now an accepted part of 'Big Wall' and expedition climbing. Mechanical devices make the task easier and faster. However they are expensive, are additional pieces of equipment to carry and, unfortunately, are liable to mechanical faults and misuse.

Jumar Clamps

These were developed by Adolf Jusi and Walter Marti in the early 1950s for climbing to eagles' nests in Switzerland. They are easy to use but the body is a die-cast alloy and has been known to fracture. Often a $1/2$ in (12 mm) tape or 7 mm rope sling is added to the Jumar body as illustrated in the sketch [b].

[b]

The clamp is fixed to the rope by depressing the safety catch. This allows the spring loaded clamp to be opened and the device fitted on to the rope. It works on a self-locking principle, the teeth on the clamp biting into the rope when load is applied. These teeth sometimes become clogged with mud or ice and the jumar is liable to slip down the rope unless the teeth are cleaned out.

If a jumar is used on a diagonal rope, ensure that the rope is parallel to the back of the clamp to enable the safety catch to lock. A small karabiner clipped on to the rope from the device will ensure that the angle is correct and prevent the jumar from twisting off the rope.

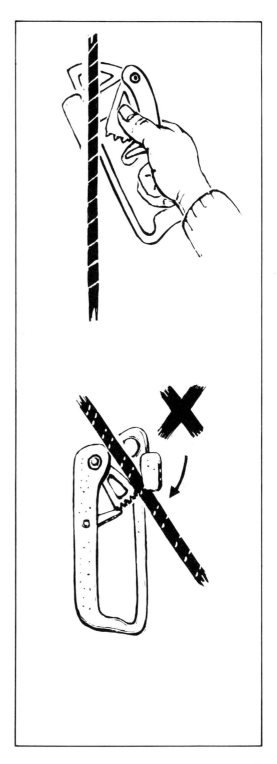

Expedition Clogger Ascendeurs
These devices are very similar to the Jumars and are
fitted to the rope in a similar fashion. The body is
made from high-strength aluminium-alloy sheet,
thus eliminating the problems associated with die-
cast alloys.

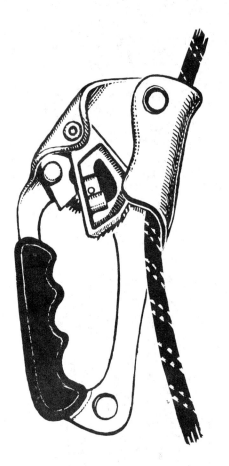
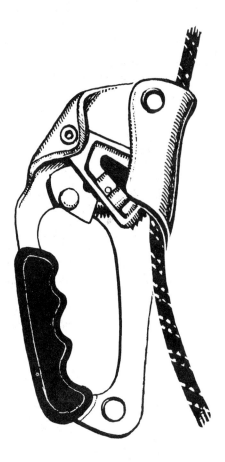

Clog Ascendeurs

The smaller clog ascendeur works on the same principle as the Jumar and the Expedition clogger. After the device has been fitted to the rope [a] a karabiner is clipped into the hole below the spring loaded clamp [b], thus preventing the clamp from opening. Although this principle is sound in theory, in practice the continual need to remove this karabiner to bypass pitons makes the operation a little tedious.

The teeth on the re-designed clamp are similar to those on the Jumar and Expedition cloggers.

Salewa Hiebeler Prusikers

These are made from a die-cast alloy, are lightweight and simple to operate, and are very effective on iced or muddy rope. To fit them, insert the rope into the top of the clamp behind the bar [c].

Squeeze the lever up against the spring [d] and slot the rope into the bottom of the clamp.

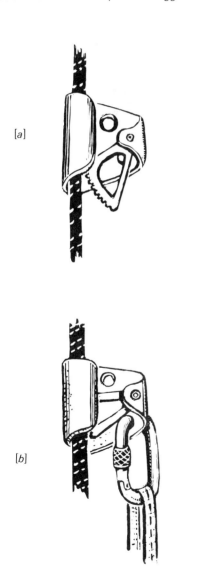

[a]

[b]

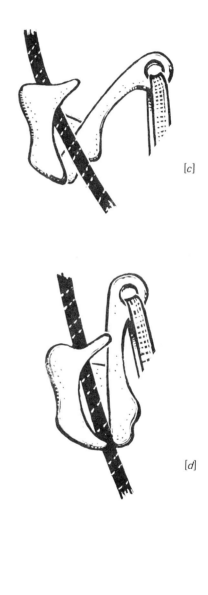

[c]

[d]

When the lever is loaded, the clamp locks on to the rope [e].

However, they do have a tendency to slip off the rope if subjected to twisting. Therefore, when pushing the device up the rope, it is advisable to keep the hand across the clamp [f]. Later models incorporate a small clip to try to prevent this but it is very flimsy and care is still necessary.

Gibbs Ascendeurs (Ropewalkers)
To fit this ascendeur to the rope [a], the quick-release pin is removed, the cam withdrawn and the rope placed in the cam housing. There is no return spring on the cam on this device so it moves up the rope very easily.

The need to remove the cam to bypass pitons and points of attachment also makes the use of this device a little tedious [b].

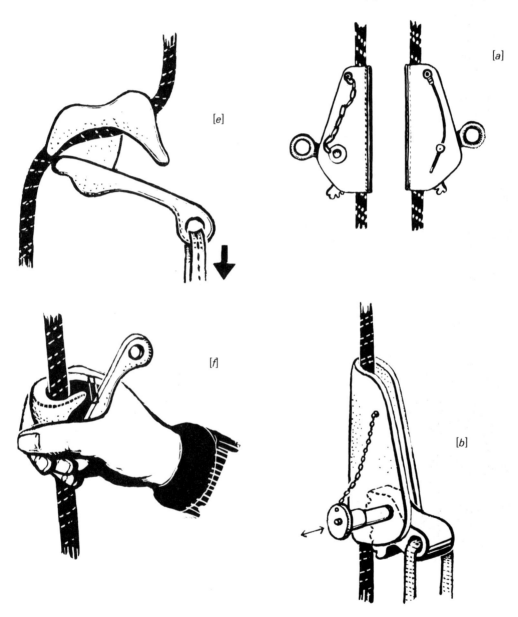

[e]

[a]

[f]

[b]

Sticht Plate for Prusiking

The sticht plate can be used for prusiking but
requires practice.

Climbing a Free Hanging Rope

The top device is attached to a linked chest and sit harness. The lower device is attached to one or both feet and a safety sling to the sit harness. All the work is done by straightening up on the foot or feet and using the very strong leg muscles [a,b, opposite].

In sketch [c], opposite, it will be seen that the climber is wearing a full body harness and the top prusik device is fitted to one foot.

These sketches serve to illustrate that there are many different ways of using prusik devices, and the climber should develop his own methods to suit a variety of situations.

Hints on Prusiking

1. Remember to attach the prusik device to your waist belt or harness.
2. If possible always tie on to the end of the prusik rope.
3. On overhangs or traverses, tie off behind the bottom device with a figure-of-eight knot, to minimise the possible length of fall.
4. Some climbers attach a prusik loop to the bottom device and attach this to the climbing rope between the devices. This way they have a back-up system should something fail.

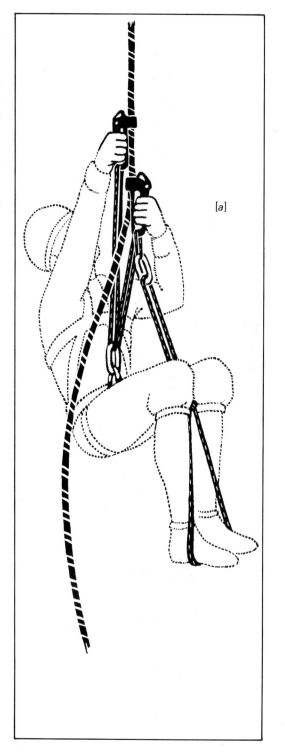

[a]

[b]

[c]

ABSEILING (*Rappeling, Roping Down*)

This is the name given to a controlled slide down a rope. It is sometimes used for descending from the top of a climb and can also be used to escape from a route which for some reason cannot be completed.

Abseiling may also be a necessary part of a climb and therefore the technique is an essential part of climbing and is worth practising.

In a practical situation the rope is used double so that it can be pulled down after the party has reached a stance and the descent continued.

There are several ways of using the rope to control the descent, and numerous special devices, known as descendeurs, have been developed.

[a]

Preliminaries

1. Select at least one anchor point. If using a flake make sure that the rope cannot roll up during the abseil. A tape sling [a] is recommended where this could happen. Ideally, the anchor point should be above the start ledge as this will make the start of the abseil easier.

    On some rock climbs, abseil slings are left in position on abseil pitches. Those should always be treated with caution. If in any doubt, add one of your own slings for absolute safety.
2. The use of a safety rope when abseiling is strongly recommended. The safety rope should be attached, if possible, to a separate anchor with the belayer adopting the normal dynamic belay position [b]. If only one rope is available, a safety rope can be arranged for all but the last man by abseiling on a single strand of rope and using the other half of the rope as a safety line.
3. When throwing the rope down, make sure that it reaches the cliff base or the ledge. A good method is to make a hand coil of about half the rope starting from the end, and tossing this down first. Then coil the remaining rope and throw that down [c, opposite].

    As a precaution, a knot is sometimes tied about 6 ft (2 m) from the end of the rope. This could save you from the embarrassment of abseiling off the end of the rope [c].

    The centre of a rope can be marked for quick identification. Do NOT use paint or dye but use a plastic adhesive tape.

[b]

[c]

The Classic Method (Dulfer)

The doubled or single rope is taken in the left hand and the climber stands astride it facing the anchor so that the rope passes between his legs from front to back. The rope is taken behind the right thigh, up and across the front of the body and over the left shoulder, front to back. The hanging rope is held in the right hand and the position of this rope controls the speed of descent. The left hand is held on the rope, purely to help balance.

The climber leans out from the cliff backwards with the legs fairly straight and the feet apart to provide a stable base. On easier-angled rock, it is helpful to turn sideways so that you can see where you are going.

On vertical rock, the climber walks backwards down the cliff. Do not let the feet remain too high, otherwise you may turn upside down. By bringing the hanging rope(s) in the right hand across the front of the body, the increased friction will slow the rate of descent. Some climbers take a turn of rope around this controlling arm to increase the friction.

DO NOT BOUNCE DOWN. It looks very spectacular but it puts great strain on the anchor. Gloves are usually worn and climbers sometimes protect the left shoulder if they do much of this type of abseiling. If you are wearing plenty of clothing, this should give sufficient protection.

If you are left-handed, then you will of course, use opposite hands.

Classic With Sit Sling (Dulfer Seat)
The basic classic method is not comfortable but has the virtue that no additional equipment is needed. However, if a sit sling is used then it makes the whole procedure more comfortable.

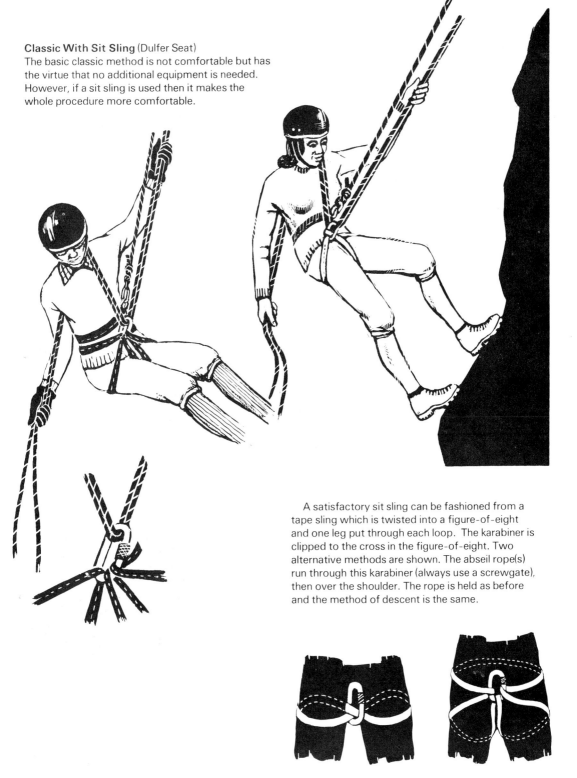

A satisfactory sit sling can be fashioned from a tape sling which is twisted into a figure-of-eight and one leg put through each loop. The karabiner is clipped to the cross in the figure-of-eight. Two alternative methods are shown. The abseil rope(s) run through this karabiner (always use a screwgate), then over the shoulder. The rope is held as before and the method of descent is the same.

A simple thigh loop clipped into the waist can also be used as a sit sling. The figure-of-eight sling, and the thigh loop can be clipped into the waist-belt, to prevent it from slipping down.

If the anchor point is low, it may be necessary to ease yourself carefully over the edge of the abseil ledge.

Descendeurs

Various metal devices have been designed to make abseiling quicker and more comfortable. However, they are extra pieces of equipment to carry and should generally be avoided, unless they are multi-purpose (e.g. the sticht plate).

Figure-of-Eight Descendeur

This device is usually referred to as a 'bottle-opener', to avoid possible confusion with the figure-of-eight knot. However, it does put a twist in the rope which is awkward on a long abseil if the end of the rope is knotted. Stand facing the anchor with your back to the cliff edge. (Your companion will of course be holding you on a safety rope throughout.) Then, pull up a bight of rope ready to push it through the large eye of the bottle-opener.

The bight or loop of rope is then passed over the shank of the device as shown [a]. The descendeur is then clipped into the waist karabiner [b] and the gate screwed up. *NEVER ABSEIL USING A NON-SCREWGATE KARABINER.*

If using a Whillans harness, check that the buckle is fastened correctly. The safety rope is best tied separately around the waist. This way you will always have an extra safeguard if your sling, belt or harness lets you down.

The descent is controlled by gripping the rope with the right hand (again assuming you are right handed) and bringing it towards the body to decrease the friction [d, opposite]. The left hand can lightly hold the rope for balance if this is felt necessary.

When threading a descendeur, make sure that the controlling rope is on the side of the device suited to you [c].

[a]

[b]

[c]

[d]

Overhangs

On small overhangs, it is usual to bounce out from the rock, descend a little, swing back in, and continue the descent.

If the anchor point is low, the abseil rope may have to be protected where it passes over a sharp edge.

Sticht Plate as a Descendeur

Basically the sticht plate was developed as a belay device, but it can be used for abseiling, and therefore is worth considering for its multi-role use.

WARNING

When using the sticht plate for abseiling it is recommended that fast abseiling is avoided, as some people feel that the build-up of heat in the plate due to friction could damage the rope.

Other Devices and Methods

Many climbers use karabiner brakes for abseiling. However, they are complicated to construct and any faulty arrangement can result in an accident.

'Racks' and 'brake bars' fitted to karabiners are also used to a lesser degree.

Protecting an Abseil

If a safety rope is not available, many climbers use a prusik loop to protect themselves during the abseil. The loop is connected to the rope above the abseil device and held in the top hand during the descent [a].

An additional karabiner can be clipped between the double abseil rope [b], as long as a knot is tied at the bottom of the abseil rope. This karabiner will prevent the climber falling off the end of the rope if he happens to lose control. (This could occur, for example, if the climber were to be hit by a falling stone.)

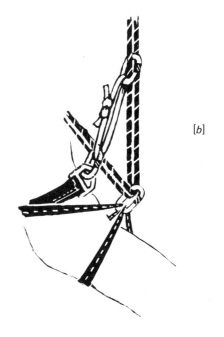

[b]

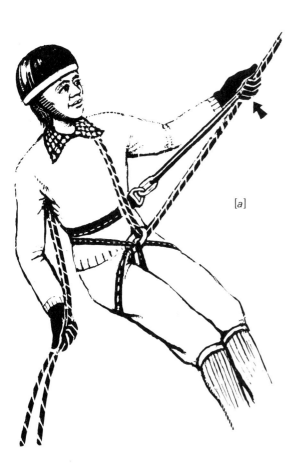

[a]

111

Joining Two Ropes

Two ropes can be joined together to provide a
longer abseil length. There are several ways of
doing this. A double fisherman's knot is normally
used, but figure-of-eight knots in each rope, joined
by a karabiner, give a satisfactory alternative.

If the abseil rope is knotted at the centre, put the
knot below the sling on the inside. When pulling the
rope down always pull the 'inside' rope. This
creates a good deal less friction at the sling.

When joining two ropes for abseiling try not to
use ropes of different diameters or construction.
This can cause problems at the anchor point due to
unequal elongation.

Finally:

A word of warning. Many highly skilled and experienced climbers have died through accidents whilst abseiling. The chief dangers are:
1. Poor anchor points.
2. Insufficient rope to reach the stance or ropes of unequal length.
3. Careless technique.

'Recollection of the West Peak' – an adaptation of A. E. Elias' illustration in an early guide book, *The Climbs on Lliwedd*, by J. M. Archer Thomson, M.A., & A. W. Andrews, M.A., published in 1909, by Edward Arnold, London, for the Climbers' Club.

Chapter Eight: Guide Books and Gradings

Guide books are available for most rock-climbing areas; their general approach is similar in most countries. They are usually of pocket size so that they can be carried conveniently on a climb. Information is given on the best way to approach the cliff, and photographs or sketches of the cliff are included to aid identification of the routes. In Britain it is also usual for the Ordnance Survey Map number to be given, together with a grid reference.

A route is named and graded by the climber doing the first ascent, and the text in the guide book will generally give information on the number of pitches, their length, general observation on the route, type of climbing, details of anchor points for belaying and the stances. Crux pitches are mentioned together with any special or unusual moves.

Details are also given on the correct descent line after completing the climb. It is important that these indicated ways down are used, as in many instances access has been negotiated with the landowner or other authority on behalf of the climbing public.

Besides giving information on the climbing, most guide books give an insight into the development of climbing in the area or cliff together with notes on the natural and geological history. Most guide books are published by climbing clubs and a few specialist commercial firms, and are usually sold in equipment shops.

GRADING OF CLIMBS

Great Britain

Climbs are graded according to their difficulty. As explained under Guide Books, the grading of the climb is initially given by the climber doing the first ascent, but this procedure is sometimes modified when an overall assessment of all the routes on a cliff is undertaken, before the publication or revision of a guide book.

It is unfortunate, but not uncommon, for a difference in grading to exist between areas, types of rock and types of climbing. Climbers visiting a new area are advised to treat gradings with caution until they are sure of their ability in that area. Climbs can alter with extensive use and a missing hold can completely alter the grading of a climb.

A TYPICAL GUIDE BOOK ROUTE DESCRIPTION

CENTRAL BUTTRESS

SPOON WALL. 120ft. Very severe. 1973. T. D. Smith and S. P. Harp.

A good route taking the right wall of Central Buttress.

Start: Between the gully and the very obvious red arête.

1. 40ft: Ascend a short rock wall to a good nut crack. Traverse diagonally right to a corner and go up to the top.

2. 80ft: Descend slightly and climb the wall on its right side to a large sloping slab. Climb the rib awkwardly to a large block and thread belay in the grassy bay.

3. 50ft: Bridge the overhanging corner, using holds on both walls to a good ledge. Climb the short wall above direct to finish with an easy mantelshelf.

Way Off: Follow the wall to the obvious gully and waymarked descent.

Note. Under a voluntary agreement with the local ornithological society, climbers are requested not to climb on this cliff from the 1st MAY to the end of JULY. Notices are posted at the foot of the crag to this effect.

Gradings should never be regarded as absolute, since so much depends on the attitude and aptitude of the climber, the weather, type of rock and other factors.

British and Continental Grading

In Britain and the Alps most climbs are graded descriptively:

EASY
(E)
A scramble where a rope is needed.

MODERATE
(MOD)
Large holds and stances on easily angled rock.

DIFFICULT
(DIFF)
Steeper climbing on good holds.

VERY DIFFICULT
(V DIFF)
Small holds on steep longer pitches. Climbing technique necessary.

SEVERE
(S)
Strenuous climbing, usually requiring previous climbing experience.

VERY SEVERE
(VS)
Sustained hard and strenuous climbing, PA type footwear preferred.

HARD VERY SEVERE
(HVS)
Harder than VS yet not hard enough to be classified as ES

EXTREMELY SEVERE
(ES)
Routes that require the ultimate in technique and strength.

In addition to the descriptive system, a numerical system for the harder climbs is finding favour. Grades range from 1 to 6 in increasing severity and are subdivided into a, b, and c. Often both systems are combined, with a descriptive grade used for the route, and a numerical grading for each individual pitch.

The Climbers' Club, in their forthcoming guides, plan to sub-divide the 'Extremely Severe' grade into five 'E' grades.

For example, the well known climb, Cenotaph Corner, on Carreg Wasted in North Wales, at the moment classified as Extremely Severe, would be graded as E1 5b.

To purchase a set of guide books for one area is very expensive these days, so to overcome this, several guide books have appeared which list a selection of the best or classic routes of different standards in the area. Sometimes a 'star rating' is applied to routes of good value, three stars, the maximum, being reserved for the great classics. If you intend to visit an area infrequently, these guide books are worth considering.

US Grading

Several grading systems are in operation; however, in Yosemite, a system is used with an overall grading of I to VI, which relates to the time needed to complete the climb, grade I usually taking about half a day, and grade VI being a multi-day climb. Technical difficulty is based on the numbers 1–5. Grade 1 is walking whilst grade 5 is serious rock climbing. This grade is further sub-divided into 1–11 (the figures after the points in the example given later). It is certain that higher numbers will be added. Artificial climbing is given the prefix A and numerals 1–5.

It is considered that grade 5.7 is about equal to the average VS in the British and continental system.

Alps

Most Alpine countries adopt the French system with minor variations, which gives an overall descriptive grade.

F   (*facile* – easy)
PD   (*peu difficile* – a little difficult)
AD   (*assez difficile* – rather difficult)
D   (*difficile* – difficult)
TD   (*très difficile* – very difficult)
ED   (*extrèmement difficile* – extremely difficult)

The suffixes 'inf.' (inférieur) or 'sup.' (supérieur) can be used to extend the range of grading. This descriptive system *does not* relate to the grades used in Britain.

A numerical grade for any rock climbing encountered is used, this being 1 to 6 with + or – for hard or mild climbing. Artificial climbing is given the prefix 'A' with four degrees of difficulty.

Australia

A numerical system ranging from 1 to 21 in increasing order of difficulty is used. A typical British HVS is reckoned to be equal to grade 17.

UIAA Climbing Classification System

It can be seen that most climbing countries, and even areas within a country, have evolved their own method of classifying or grading climbs, all of which are quite controversial. In an effort to overcome this, the UIAA have suggested a Climbing Classification System based on six grades, Roman numerals 1–VI, for free climbing, with the addition of plus and minus beginning at Grade III, which gives 14 separate grades. Artificial grades are given the symbol A, with numbers 0 to 4.

Comparative Chart of Grading

UIAA	Britain	US Decimal
I Easy	Easy	1
II Moderate	Moderate	2 and 3
III −		4.0
III Moderate difficulty	Difficult/very 2a 2b difficult 3a 3b	5.0
III +		5.1
IV −		5.2
IV Difficult	Severe 4a	5.3
IV +		5.4
V −		5.5
V Very difficult	Very severe 4b 4c 5a	5.6
V +		5.7
VI −		5.8
VI Extremely difficult	Hard, very 5a to severe and 6b upwards	5.9
VI +		5.10

Comparison of Grading Systems

Whether this proposed system will eventually be accepted by the majority of climbers is questionable – only time will tell. Most classification systems have evolved to take account of national and local conditions and thinking. It is also inevitable that overlapping of grading will take place. The UIAA have also proposed a series of conventional signs for rock climbing descriptions.

A note on the BRITISH MOUNTAINEERING COUNCIL

The British Mountaineering Council, founded in 1944, is constituted to foster and promote the interests of British mountaineers and mountaineering in the United Kingdom and overseas. Jointly with the Mountaineering Council of Scotland it is the representative body of British mountaineers. Full membership is open to mountaineering clubs and organisations whose principal objects are mountaineering, who have headquarters in the United Kingdom and who are owned and controlled by their members. Associate membership is open to bodies who do not qualify for full membership and to individuals.

The work of the BMC includes assisting member clubs and, with their co-operation, improving facilities such as guide books, huts, reciprocal rights in club huts, ensuring adequate training for novice mountaineers, resisting encroachments on the mountain environment, negotiating access rights for mountain areas, outcrops and sea cliffs and helping expeditions overseas in co-operation with the Mount Everest Foundation and the Alpine Club. The testing of a wide range of equipment is organised. Advice on mountaineering matters is given to a wide variety of organisations. In co-operation with the Mountaineering Council of Scotland, the BMC provides a British Mountain Guide qualification for experienced mountaineers who wish to perform as mountain guides in Britain.

BMC publications cover many aspects of mountaineering. They include guide books, safety handbooks, pamphlets and posters, equipment, information and advice. Sets of safety filmstrips or slides covering summer and winter mountaineering are available and in preparation are slide sets on basic and advanced rock climbing. For information apply to: **The Assistant Secretary, British Mountaineering Council, Crawford House, Precinct Centre, Manchester University, Booth Street East, Manchester. Telephone: 061-273 5835.**

GLOSSARY

Abseil (Rope Down/ Rappel/AB Off) — Controlled slide down a rope, usually doubled.

Aid — Artificially introduced hold.

Aid Climbing (Artificial or Peg Climbing) — Climbing which relies on pitons and bolts to make progress.

Bachmann Knot — Sophisticated version of the prusik knot, incorporating a karabiner.

Back Rope — Method of rope management to safeguard a climber across a traverse.

Backing — Method of chimney climbing.

Backing Off — Abandoning a climb.

Belay, Dynamic — Method of holding the rope to safeguard the ascending climber.

Belay, Static — Method used to anchor the belaying climber to the rock face.

Bivouac (Bivvy) — Spend the night on a mountain side or rock face, by design or involuntarily.

Bolts — Expansion bolts, used in aid climbing.

Bomb — Colloquialism, meaning to move quickly.

Bouldering — Practice of climbing on boulders.

Bridging — Method of climbing wide chimneys.

Cairn — Man-made pile of stones often used to mark the start of a route, or way off a mountain or a summit point.

Calls — Verbal communication between climbers, whilst on a route.

Capstone — Flat chockstone at the top of a chimney or gulley.

Chalk — French chalk is used by climbers to enable a more positive grip to be obtained on a small holds. (The practice has received criticism when used on easy graded climbs.)

Chimney — Crack wide enough to admit the whole body.

Chockstone (Chock) — Boulder, stone or pebble jammed in a crack. Also a specially machined shape of metal or plastic, used as an artificial chockstone.

Choss (Chossy) — Colloquialism for a loose or dirty climb.

Classic (Route or Climb) — Often the most interesting and typical route on the crag.

Climbing Wall — Man-made wall used for practising climbing techniques.

Crack — Fissure in a rock face varying in width.

Crux — Hardest part of the climb.

Delicate Climbing — Opposite of strenuous climbing, often requiring more balance than strength.

Descendeur — Metal friction device used in abseiling.

Dodaro — UIAA standard for climbing ropes.

Ethics — Code of practice in climbing.

Etriers — Three-rung ladder used in climbing.

Exposure — Climber's awareness or feeling of height — this will vary with individuals. Also suggestive of the medical condition indicating fatigue, cold etc: hypothermia.

Fall Factor — Amount of energy which a rope can absorb, depending on the length between the falling climber and his belay.

Flake — Thin piece of rock usually partly detached from the rock face.

Free Climbing — Opposite of artificial or aid climbing.

Gabbro — Extremely rough rock of the granite family.

Gangway — Sloping ledge.

Glacis — Sloping area of rock up to 30°.

Grading of climbs — Any system used to classify climbs into standards according to difficulty.

Granite — An igneous rock.

Greasy Rock — Term used to describe rock which is slippery when wet.

Gripped — Colloquialism for 'frightened'.

Gritstone — A course-grained sedimentary rock.

Groove — V-shaped fissure in a rock-face.

Guide — Professional mountaineer who takes clients on climbs.

Guide Book — Book giving descriptions of rock climbs.

Gully (Couloir) — Deep cleft in a mountain-side or rock face; usually a natural watercourse.

Hand Traverse — Horizontal movement across a rock face, supported mainly by the hands.

Hard Man — Someone who climbs at a high standard.

Harness — Piece of equipment for attaching the rope to the climber, so that shock loads, in the event of a fall, will be broadly distributed over the whole body. It should also ensure that in the event of a fall the climber is held in a sitting position.

Holds	Rock features which the climber uses as foot and hand holds.
Holster	A stiff nylon or plastic tube attached to a belt or harness to hold a piton hammer.
Jamming	Climbing technique where the hands and feet are wedged in cracks.
Jumar Clamps	Mechanical devices for prusiking, or climbing up the rope.
Karabiner (Mousqueton/Snap-link)	Usually, an oval or 'D' shaped metal link with a spring-loaded gate on one side. On some models, this gate can be secured by a screwed sleeve.
Kernmantel (Sheath & Core)	Type of rope construction.
Kletterschuh	Lightweight climbing boot, originally having a felt sole.
Layback (Lie-back/ A La Dulfer)	A strenuous crack-climbing technique.
Leader	First climber on a rope.
Ledge	Relatively flat surface on a cliff face.
Leeper	A 'Z'-shaped, hard-steel piton developed in the US.
Limestone	A sedimentary rock.
Line	Route taken by a climb.
Mantelshelf (Chinning)	Technique in climbing used to gain a high ledge.
Niche	Small recess in a rock-face.
Nuts	Colloquialism for artificial chock stones.
Outcrop	Crag or group of crags which jut out from a hill or mountain side.
Overhang	Rock face which juts out beyond the vertical.
PA's	Lightweight climbing boots with a smooth rubber sole, developed by Pierre Allain.
Peel	Colloquialism for falling off a climb.
Peg	Piton.
Peg Hammer	Hammer for driving pitons.
Pendule (Pendulum)	Swinging motion on a rope to gain sideways movement across holdless rock.
Pitch	Section of climb between two stances on a rock climb.
Pocket	Small hollow in a rock face usually used as a handhold.
Protection	General term used to describe the method used by a climber to safeguard himself.
Prusiking	Technique of climbing a rope.
Reverse	Climb down.
Rib	Short, steep rock ridge.
Ridge (Crest)	Line on which two faces of a mountain meet.
Roof	Underside of a large (horizontal) overhang.
Rope Walkers	Mechanical devices, or prusikers, used for climbing a rope.
Route	Overall direction taken by a climb.
Rubbers	Colloquialism for gym shoes.
Run Out	Length of rope on a pitch between the leader and the second.
Runner	A running belay.
Safety Rope	Separate rope used to protect a climber, usually whilst abseiling.
Scoop	Rounded niche in a rock face.
Scree (Talus)	Boulders and small stones covering a steep slope.
Sky Hook (Bat Hook)	Flattened hook used as an aid in advanced climbing.
Slab	Flat area of inclined rock.
Sling	Loop of rope or tape used for belaying, abseiling, running belays, etc.
Solo	Climbing alone.
Stance	Place to stand or sit and belay.
Sticht Plate	An auto-belaying device.
Swami Belt	Type of waist tie used in the US.
Tape	Usually refers to nylon tape of various widths and constructions.
Thin	Term meaning delicate and difficult climbing.
Thread	Type of belay.
Top Rope	Protection for the climber by a rope usually held from above.
Traverse	Horizontal section on a climb.
Tying On	Method of attaching the climbing rope to the body.
Tyrolean	Method of crossing a gap by using a rope.
UIAA	Union Internationale des Associations d'Alpinisme.
Vibram Sole	Type of cleated rubber sole.
Wall	Rock face greater than 75°.

Index

Abseiling, 102
  anchor points, 102
  bottle openers, 108
  brake bars, 110
  classic, 104
  descendeurs, 107
  joining two ropes, 112
  overhangs, 110
  practice, 102
  protecting the abseil, 111
  racks, 110
  safety rope, 102
  sticht plate, 110
  thigh loop, 105, 106
  throwing the rope down, 102, 103
  with sit sling, 105
Aid, 79
Anchor, 61
  chockstone, 65
  flake, 62
  piton, 67
  selection, 61
  spike, 62
  thread, 66
Arête, 31
Auto belayers, 74

Backing up, 50
Basic climbing principles, 26
  standing upright, 26
  position of the hands, 27
  testing all holds, 27
  thinking ahead, 27
  three points of contact, 26
Belaying, 61
  belay practice device, 77
  changing over, 70
  chockstones, 65
  definition, 61
  dynamic, 61, 68
  escape from the system, 72
  flake, 62
  holding a fall, 72
  loop, 63
  paying out the rope, 71
  rope slings, 63
  running belays, 73, 76
  second to continue, 70
  selecting anchors, 61
  sitting, 67, 68
  spike, 62
  sticht plate, 74

taking in the rope, 69
  tape, 62
  threads, 66
  three on a rope, 73
  trees, 64
Belts, 13, 14
British Mountaineering Council, 118
Boots
  climbing boots, 11
  PA's, 11
  kletterschuhe, 12
  vibram soles, 11
Bouldering, 25
Bowline, 53
Braking arm, 75
Braking effect, 72
Breaking strain of rope, 17
Breeches, 22
Bridging, 50

Cable rope, 17
Calls, 37–40
Chest tie, 16
Chimneys, 30, 49
  backing, 50
  bridging, 50
  wriggling, 50
Chockstones
  basic types, 86
  belaying, 79
  carrying, 90, 91
  manufactured, 86
  other materials, 86
  pebbles, 85
  placing, 89
  removal, 90
  rope, 88
  tape, 88
  wire, 86
Classic abseil, 104
Climbing down, 42
Climbing sequence, 35
Climbing wall, 25
Clothing, 22
Clove hitch, 59
Clubs, 115
Coiling the rope, 18
Combined holds, 51
Communication in bad weather, 41
Controlling arm, 108
Core and sheath rope, 17 (see also
  Kernmantel rope)

Corner, 30
Cracks, 29
  arm jamming, 48
  finger jamming, 48
  fist jamming, 48
  hand jamming, 48
  knee jamming, 51
Crux, 115

Descendeurs, 107
  figure of eight, 107
  karabiner brakes, 110
  racks, 110
  sticht plates, 110
Descending, 42
Double fisherman's knot, 55

Equipment, 11
  types, 23
  costs, 11

Falling leaders, 36, 72
FB's, 11
Features of a rock face, 28
  arêtes, 31
  corners, 30
  chimneys, 30
  cracks, 29
  glacis, 28
  grooves, 31
  gullies, 30
  overhangs, 29
  ribs, 31
  slabs, 28
  stances, 31
  walls, 29
Figure-of-eight
  descendeurs, 107, 108
  knots, 54
Finger jams, 48
Fist jams, 48
Flake belays, 62
Foot jam, 51
Foot loop, 93
Footholds, 50

Gabbro, 33
Glacis, 28
Gloves, 68
Grading, 115, 116
  Alps, 116
  Australia, 116

comparison of grades, 116
Great Britain, 115, 116
UIAA, 116
USA, 116
Groove, 31
Guide books, 115
typical route description, 115
Gully, 30
Gymshoes, 11

Hammers, 21, 82
Handholds, 45
finger holds, 45
flat holds, 45
incut holds, 45
jughandles, 45
layback, 47
mantelshelf, 46
pinchgrip, 47
pressure holds, 45
side pulls, 47
undercut holds, 47
Hand jam, 48
Hand traversing, 49
Hard steel pitons, 80
Harnesses, 13
body
improvised chest, 16
sit (Troll/Whillans), 15
Hawser-laid rope, 17
Helmets, 12
Hitch (two half), 55
Holster, 21

Inactive rope, 69
Incut holds, 45

Jammed nuts, 85
chockstones, 86
machine nuts, 86
Jams
arm, 48
finger, 48
fist, 48
hand, 48
knee, 51
Joining two ropes, 55, 56, 112
Jug handle, 45
Jumars, 94

Karabiners, 19
hints on use, 20
screwgate, 19
UIAA, 19
Kernmantel rope, 17

Kletterschuhe, 12
Knee jamming, 51
Knots, 53
bachmann, 58
bowline, 53
clove hitch, 59
double fisherman's, 55
double loop bowline, 53
figure of eight, 54
klemheist, 58
overhand or thumb, 55
prusik, 57
sheetbend, 56
stopper, 55
tape, 56
two half hitches, 55

Laybacking, 47
Lark's foot, 93
Leader, 43
fall, 36, 72
leading down, 42
leading through, 35, 70
protection, 36
traverse, 73
Ledge, 28
Limestone, 32
Live rope, 68
Loose rock, 27, 41

Mantelshelf, 46
Melting point of rope, 17

Nuts, 21, 85
Nylon, 16

Outcrop, 32
Overhand knot, 55
Overhangs, 29

PAs, 11
Pinch grip, 47
Pitch, 73, 115
Pitons, 79
angles, 81
bongs, 81
carrying, 84
design, 79
driving, 83
ethics, 79
hard steel, 80
horizontal, 80
leepers, 81
other materials, 80
other types, 82

placing, 83
practice, 84
removal, 84
shapes, 80
sizes, 80
soft steel, 79
stacking, 84
tying off, 83
vertical, 80
Pressure hold, 45
Protection, 36
Prusiking, 93
classic method, 93
climbing a free hanging rope, 100
clog ascendeurs, 97
expedition cloggers, 96
Gibb ascendeurs, 98
jumar clamps, 94
mechanical devices, 94
safety, 100
salewa/hiebeler prusikers, 97
sticht plate for prusiking, 99

Rappel see abseil
Rib, 31
Rock types, 32
gabbro, 33
granite, 33
gritstone, 32
limestone, 32
rhyolite, 33
sandstone, 32
Rope and rope management, 16
abseiling, 102
bight, 63, 74
breaking strain, 17
care of the rope, 19
carrying the rope, 16, 18
choosing the rope, 17
climbing down, 42
coiling the rope, 18
dead (inactive) rope, 69
hawser-laid, 17
kernmantel, 17
live (active) rope, 68
melting point, 17
paying out, 71
pulling down the rope, 112
roping down (abseil), 102
sling, 20
storage, 17
taking in, 38
three climbing, 73
throwing down the rope, 41
top roping, 42

tying on, 13
Route descriptions, 115
Running belays, 36

Safety rope, 102
Screwgate karabiner, 19
Second man, 35, 70
Sheetbend, 56
Side pull, 47
Sky hook, 82
Slab, 28
Slings, 20
  care, 20
  carrying, 20
  rope, 20
  tape, 20
Stance, 31
Sticht plate, 74
Standards, 34, 114 (*see also* Grading)
Stopper knots, 55
Study of leaders, 43

Swami, 14

Tape, 20
  knots, 56
  slings, 20
Techniques, 45
  back and foot, 49
  backing up, 50
  bridging, 50
  finger jam, 48
  fist jam, 48
  hand jam, 48
  jumaring, 93
  layback, 47
  leading through, 70
  mantelshelf, 46
  prusiking, 93
  straddling, 50
  wriggling, 49
Thread belay, 66
Top roping, 42

Trees, 64
Tying off, 72, 73
Tying on, 13

UIAA, 17
Undercut hold, 47

Vibram rubber soles, 11

Waist ties, 13
  belts, 13
  sit harnesses, 15
  swami belts, 14
Walls, 29
  artificial climbing, 25
  rock, 29
What to learn, 26
Where to learn, 25
Wire slings, 21, 86
Wriggling, 49

NOTES

NOTES

NOTES

NOTES